THE
JOYFUL SPIRIT
OF
PADRE PIO

Stories, Letters, and Prayers

PATRICIA TREECE

Compiled by the Editors of Servant Books

SERVANT
BOOKS

PUBLISHED BY FRANCISCAN MEDIA
Cincinnati, Ohio

Cover design by Paul Higdon | Book design by Mark Sullivan

LIBRARY OF CONGRESS CATALOGING-IN-PUBLICATION DATA
Treece, Patricia.
  The joyful spirit of Padre Pio : stories, letters, and prayers / Patricia Treece ; compiled by the editors of Servant Books.
    pages cm
  Includes bibliographical references.
  ISBN 978-1-61636-732-9 (alk. paper)
  1. Pio, of Pietrelcina, Saint, 1887-1968. I. Title.
  BX4700.P7755T737 2014
  271'.3602—dc23
                                        2014016015
ISBN 978-1-61636-732-9

Printed in the United States of America.
Printed on acid-free paper.
14 15 16 17 18   5 4 3 2 1

Contents

Who Is Padre Pio?

ON THE ONE HAND, THE eighty-three-year-old Capuchin in his remote southern Italian friary was venerated so widely that his death in September 1968 was reported even in non-Catholic countries. The news appeared in the most important English-language media of that day, *The London Times* and *The New York Times*.

On the other hand, even though he has been a canonized saint since 2002, people periodically try to expose Pio as being "a fake mystic with self-created stigmata wounds." Other analysts, including Catholics, who do not believe he is a phony, nevertheless reduce Pio to a very pious soul with a limited neurosis that made him bleed.

Those who wish to know the truth about him will be glad to know that the Church has a centuries old tradition of rigorous investigation of highly out-of-the ordinary conditions, events, and people in its ranks. Because his life was unusual in all three ways, Pio underwent a number of investigations during his lifetime as to who and what he was—mystic or fake, well-balanced or neurotic.

As God's friend, he swallowed his embarrassed repugnance and let men of science, including nonbelievers, examine his wounds in studies sponsored by branches of the Church (including his own order and popes). Others, like a non-believing, well-known journalist who was naively given access to Pio when his stigmata were first becoming known, made their own reports. His was favorable, having seen "an impossible" cure before his eyes.

Lifelong informal observation by Pio's superiors and spiritual directors was followed by the post-death, pre-canonization investigation. No Catholic gets held up as a role model for following Christ until his life has been examined with a fine-tooth comb. Truly heroic virtues had better balance oddities like the stigmata.

This book and my previous ones are based on my research mentored by Father Joseph Pius Martin (d. 2000), Pio's spiritual son, who provided authentic materials and introductions to those who knew Pio or received God's miracles through him.

Because of all these trustworthy sources, I assure you Padre Pio was a man who had such a profound relationship with God that his whole life revealed the divine, changing people's lives. He was also a down-to-earth human being who loved to tease his fellow Capuchins and friends.

Yes, he drew people fascinated with the mysterious and awesome in spirituality or, if they lacked even the slightest spiritual foundation, with what they found magical or bizarre.

Such people focused on the wounds like Christ's that Pio did his best to hide, his living inexplicably without normal nourishment or sleep, "odors of sanctity" that sometimes announced his unseen presence, or visible bilocations.

To those who come to know him, even through mass media, these things eventually recede, as do the analyses of writers, doctors, and psychiatrists who have tried to "explain" Padre Pio. Instead what emerges is "a simple friar who prays," tenderly compassionate and other-directed, a man able to joke even in a long dark night of the soul where God protected Pio's humility by hiding Pio's holiness from himself, leaving him uncertain whether God approved of him or not.

Who knows you like your family? In these pages, along with those he ministered to and his parish priest, you will find his Capuchin family—his teachers and spiritual directors, Pio's own students and spiritual directees, novices and mature friary mates he lived with for decades. They witness neither to Pio's perfection nor to his extraordinary spiritual gifts so much as to the richness of his love, especially forbearance for each of them—and for all.

Turn the page; read and see for yourself.

• ONE •

God's Love and Mercy

AN IRISH WOMAN WAS TOLD she should seek the intercession of Pio for her tiny dying daughter. Surely, she thought, this man—reputed to read hearts and know one's sins—must be severe, willing to help only the practically perfect. But when, in desperation, she turned to Pio for prayer, her child's defective heart was replaced by God with a perfect one.[1] This mother, like many, discovered that Padre Pio is all about God's tender love and mercy.

Loving mercy toward others grew out of the saint's passionate relationship with God, who is Love. As Pio grew year after

---

1. Interviewed in 1987 for *Nothing Short of a Miracle,* about Pio's healing appearance, the woman and her now-adult daughter were re-interviewed for the book's 2013 edition.

year in holiness, he more and more mediated to others the love that set his heart ablaze. To this day, his compassion spreads out like a warming quilt over all within his reach.

The Fires of Love

PIO WAS ONE OF THE mystics who burn, even physically, with love for God. In his letters to his spiritual directors, he sometimes writes about this:

> I feel my heart and my inmost being completely absorbed by the mounting flames of an immense fire. These flames cause my poor soul to give vent to pitiful laments. Yet who would believe it? While my soul experiences an atrocious agony caused by the flames I have described, it is filled at the same time by an exceeding sweetness which calls forth immense love of God.

The flames of divine love burned but did not consume Pio:

> I feel myself annihilated, dear Father, and I cannot find anywhere to hide from this gift of the Divine Master. I am sick with an illness of the heart. I cannot go on any longer. The thread of life seems ready to break from one moment to the next, yet this moment never comes.

My dear Father, the soul is in a sad state when God has made it sick with His love.

Years later, he recalled that when saying Mass:

It seems to me at times that it [my heart] must burst out of my chest. Sometimes at the altar my whole body burns in an indescribable manner. My face, in particular, seems to go on fire.

He felt unable to "pour out this ever-active volcano which burns me up and which Jesus has placed in this very small heart. It can all be summed up as follows: I am consumed by love for God and love for my neighbor. God is constantly fixed in my mind and imprinted on my heart. I never lose sight of Him."

All about Love

PADRE EUSEBIO, WHO WAS ABOUT twenty-seven, had been sent to Ireland to study English so he could assist Padre Pio with his correspondence in this language. Upon his return, Padre Eusebio was helping Pio in the latter's cell when Padre Pio suddenly said he wanted to go to confession. Feeling his youthful lack of experience, Padre Eusebio wanted to beg off, worrying, "What if he asks me something about mystical theology?" But Padre Pio launched into the penitent's opening prayer: "Bless me, Father, for I have sinned," and the young friar was stuck. To Padre Eusebio's surprise, Padre Pio, as he confessed, burst out weeping.

Immediately, Padre Eusebio wanted to console Pio that he had not done anything so bad but Padre Pio countered, "Listen, my son, you think, like many others, that sin is the breaking of the law, but it's not that but infidelity to love."

Advice on Loving God

YOU ARE TRYING TO MEASURE, understand, feel, and touch the love which you have for God. But, my dear sister, you must accept as certain that the more a soul loves God, the less it feels this love....

God is incomprehensible and inaccessible; hence the more a soul penetrates into the love of this Supreme Good, the more the sentiment of love towards him, which is beyond the soul's knowledge, seems to diminish, until the poor soul considers that it no longer loves him at all.

In certain instances it seems to the soul that this is really the case but that continual fear, that holy circumspection which makes one look carefully where to place one's feet so as not to stumble, that courage in facing the assaults of the enemy, that resignation to God's will in all life's adversities, that ardent desire to see God's kingdom established in one's own heart and in the hearts of others are the clearest proof of the soul's love [for God].

Living in God's Love

Love never ends.

—1 CORINTHIANS 13:8

MAY JESUS FILL YOU WITH his holy love, and may he transform you totally in him!

May our most sweet Savior [remove] your heart, as he did with his servant St. Catherine of Siena, in order to grant you his most divine heart, through which you can then live totally of his holy love.

Prescription: Boundless Confidence in God's Mercy

AT TIMES THE SPIRIT IS willing and the flesh weak, but God wants the spirit more than anything else. Cling closer and closer to him, then, with your will, with the highest point of your soul. Let nature feel [the suffering], and be roused to demand its rights, for nothing is more natural. If nature is also subjected to suffering at present, this is not due to itself, for nature too was made for happiness. These sufferings are due to it because of sin. What criminal is there who, when subjected to what he recognizes as deserved...does not feel the pain and demand to be freed from it?

Always bear in mind as a safe general rule that while God tries us by his crosses and sufferings, he always leaves us a glimmer of light by which we continue to have great trust in him and to recognize his immense goodness. I urge you, therefore, not to be entirely disheartened in the face of the cross... heaven bestows on you, but to continue to have boundless confidence in the divine mercy.

The Spirit of God Is a Spirit of Peace

THE SPIRIT OF GOD IS a spirit of peace. Even in the most serious faults he makes us feel a sorrow that is tranquil, humble, and confident and this is precisely because of his mercy.

The spirit of the devil, instead, excites, exasperates, and makes us feel, in that very sorrow, anger against ourselves, whereas we should on the contrary be charitable with ourselves first and foremost.

Therefore if any thought agitates you, this agitation never comes from God, who gives you peace, being the Spirit of Peace, but from the devil.

Let God Bury Our Sins

O come, let us worship and bow down,
  let us kneel before the LORD, our Maker!

—PSALM 95:6

DURING THE RIOTING OF THE passions and adverse events, keep in mind the dear hope of his unlimited mercy. Let us run with confidence to the tribunal of penance, where he waits for you at all times with the anxiety of a father; and although we are conscious of our debt towards him, let us not doubt the solemn pardon of our sins. Let us bury them as our Lord has done.

Mercy Grants Glory

So we do not lose heart. Though our outer nature is wasting away, our inner nature is being renewed every day. For this slight momentary affliction is preparing for us an eternal weight of glory beyond all comparison, because we look not to the things that are seen but to the things that are unseen; for the things that are seen are transient, but the things that are unseen are eternal.

—2 Corinthians 4:16–18

I...always bring pressure to bear on the heart of the heavenly Father for [your sister] Giovina's health, and also for your own.... However, I must tell you for your own comfort that a complete cure of the disease from which poor Giovina is suffering would not be for God's glory, for the salvation of her soul, and [for] the edification of those who live according to the spirit of Jesus Christ. Hence I cannot insist, I cannot demand from the divine Heart to grant her this favor. I will certainly pray and never forget it, since this is the Lord's will, wherever I am and no matter in what state I may be, that the Lord may be pleased to grant her constantly at least the degree of holiness necessary for the fulfillment of her duties....

11

I am confident that the Lord God, who is so good to his creatures, will not refuse the poor prayer of his servant. In fact, I hope he will grant more grace...than I dare to ask.

The other reason why I refrain from asking [for] a complete cure for Giovina is because this illness is, for her, a most powerful means of practicing many virtues. I cannot deprive this generous soul, who is so dear to Jesus, of such great treasures through a mistaken sense of pity and affection for you.

Love and the Sick

Love is patient and kind.

—1 CORINTHIANS 13:4

PADRE PIO FOUNDED A HOSPITAL called the Home for the Relief of Suffering, which today sits directly across from the friary. On May 6, 1956, the day the hospital was officially opened, Padre Pio exhorted the doctors who work there:

> You have the mission of curing the sick; but if you don't bring love to the sickbed, I don't think the medicines will be of much use. I have experienced this:... When I was ill in 1916–17, my doctor, when curing me, first of all gave me a word of comfort. Love cannot manage without words. How can you express it if not with words that relieve the sick person spiritually? Bring God to the patients; it will be of more worth than any other cure.

Lord, when I help someone who is ill, let me never forget that love is the most important medicine. And when I am ill, Lord, please send me medical men and women who are not only wise and skilled but filled with love.

The Surest Sign of Love

HOW SWEET IS THE WORD "cross"! Here at the foot of Jesus' cross souls are clothed in light and inflamed with love; here they acquire wings to bear them upward in loftiest flight. May the same cross always be our bed of rest, our school of perfection, our beloved heritage.

For this reason we must never separate the cross from Jesus' love; otherwise it would become a weight which in our weakness we could not carry. May the Sorrowful Virgin obtain for us from her most holy Son the grace to penetrate more deeply into the mystery of the cross and like her to become inebriated with Jesus' sufferings. The surest sign of love is the capacity to suffer for the beloved, and since the Son of God endured many sufferings for pure love, there is no doubt that the cross carried for him becomes as lovable as love itself.

Keep Your Eyes on the Lord

To you I lift up my eyes,
 O you who are enthroned in the heavens!
Behold, as the eyes of servants
 look to the hand of their master,
as the eyes of a maid
 to the hand of her mistress,
so our eyes look to the LORD our God,
 till he have mercy upon us.

—PSALM 123:1–2

WE NEED DO NO MORE than we are doing at present; that is, to love divine Providence and abandon ourselves in his arms and heart.

Lord, just for today let the eyes of my heart never stray from your face.

How to Love God More

We love, because he first loved us.

—1 JOHN 4:19

I IMPLORE YOU BY THE meekness of our divine Master not to let yourself be overcome by that fear which is apparent to me from your letter—that is, the fear of not loving God....

I know, my dearest daughter, that no soul can worthily love God. But when this soul does everything possible and trusts in divine mercy, why should Jesus reject it? Doesn't he... command us to love God in accordance with our strength, and not as he deserves? Therefore, if you have given and consecrated everything to God, why do you fear? Perhaps because you can do no more? But Jesus doesn't ask that of you....

On the other hand, tell our good God to do himself what you cannot do. Say to Jesus: Do you want more love from me? I have no more! Give me some more, and I'll offer it to you!

Do not doubt. Jesus will accept the offer.

Loving the Dear God

God is love, and he who abides in love abides in God, and
God abides in him.

—1 JOHN 4:16

And we know that the Son of God has come and has given us
understanding, to know him who is true; and we are in him
who is true, in his Son Jesus Christ. This is the true God and
eternal life.

—1 JOHN 5:20

WORDS ARE LACKING BY WHICH to give even a feeble descrip-
tion of what passes between my soul and God.... The things
which are taking place at present are so secret and private that
anyone who has not himself experienced them could never,
never form even a faint idea of them.

What my soul receives in this state is received in a very
different manner from previously. It is now God himself who
acts and operates directly in the depths of my soul, without
the ministry of the senses, either interior or exterior. This is,
in a word, such a sublime, secret, and sweet operation that it is

concealed from all human creatures and even from the intelligence of the rebellious angels.

In this state my soul is happy, for it feels it loves its dear God and at the same time experiences his love in a very delicate way. All I can say of this…is that my soul has no concern for anything but God. I feel my whole being concentrated and recollected in God.

Love of the Beloved

DEAR FATHER, I FEEL I am drowned in the immense ocean of the love of my Beloved. I am being surfeited continually with it. Yet the bitterness of this love has a sweetness, and its burden is light, but this does not prevent my soul from feeling the immense transport of this love. I have no means to bear its immense weight, so that I feel annihilated and vanquished. My small heart is incapable of containing this immense love. It is true that it is inside and outside me. But, dear God, when you pour yourself into the little vase of my being, I suffer the agony of not being able to contain you. The inner walls of this heart feel as if they were about to burst, and I am surprised this has not happened already.

Cast out Fear, in Real Love

If we earnestly endeavor to love Jesus, this alone will drive all fear from our hearts, and the soul will find that instead of walking in the Lord's paths, it is flying. The soul in this state is induced to exclaim with the royal prophet: I will run in the way of thy commandments when thou enlargest my understanding! (Psalm 119:32).

Love, Lord, is a word bandied left and right, used to sell cosmetics and send young men to die for country. The more I ponder what love is—the heights and depths, the boundlessness of real love— the more I see its glory and its cost. That glory is you, Lord, who are Love. Real love, the kind you lived and still model both in yourself and your saints like Pio, is the pearl of great price that can only be had by selling everything.

To Love God, Our True Good

THE FIRST VIRTUE REQUIRED BY the person who is striving for perfection is charity. In all natural things the first movement, the first inclination or impulse, is to tend toward the center, in obedience to a physical law. The same thing happens in the supernatural sphere; the first movement of our hearts is a movement toward God, which is nothing more than loving our own true good. With good reason Sacred Scripture speaks of charity as the bond of perfect harmony.

Charity has as its close relatives joy and peace. Joy is born of happiness at possessing what we love. Now, from the moment at which the soul knows God, it is naturally led to love him. If the soul follows this natural impulse, which is caused by the Holy Spirit, it is already loving the Supreme Good. This fortunate soul…possesses the beautiful virtue of love. By loving God the soul is certain of possessing him. When a person loves money, honors, and good health, unfortunately he does not always possess what he loves, whereas he who loves God possesses him at once.

The Fire of Love

I NO SOONER BEGIN TO pray than my heart is filled with a fire of love. This fire does not resemble any fire on this lowly earth. It is a delicate and very gentle flame which consumes without causing any pain. It is so sweet and delightful that it satisfies and satiates my spirit to the point of insatiability. Dear God! This is a wonderful thing for me, something I will perhaps never understand until I get to heaven.

[My] desire [for God] is not extinguished by the delight experienced, but is rather perfected by this delight.

God's Love and Human Ingratitude

WHEN I CONSIDER JESUS' LOVE on the one hand and my own ingratitude on the other, my dear Father, I should like to tell him that if I cannot correspond to his love he should stop loving me; only in this way do I feel less guilty. But if Jesus does not love me, what is to become of me? Not to love Jesus and not to be loved any more by him! This is too terrifying a thing for me, and hence it makes me invariably pray Jesus to continue to love me and to help me himself if I do not succeed in loving him as much as he deserves.

Holy and Unholy Fears

THERE IS THE FEAR OF God and the fear of Judas. Too much fear makes us act without love, and too much confidence [presumption] causes us not to consider and fear the danger that we must overcome. One should help the other, and go together like two sisters. Always, when we become aware of being afraid, of having too much fear, we should remember to become confident. If we are excessively confident, we should become instead a little fearful. Love tends to the object loved; however, in its approach, it is blind. But holy fear enlightens it.

Love Is from God

YOU BECOME SAD AT THE little love you feel for God. It seems to you that it is little more than nothing.... But...don't you yourself feel this love in your soul? What is that doubt, or rather, what is that ardent desire that you yourself express to me?

Well, you should know...that *in divino* that desire to love is love. Who placed this yearning to love the Lord in your heart? Don't holy desires come from above? Are we perhaps capable of arousing in ourselves one single desire of that kind without the grace of God, which sweetly works within us? If there is nothing but the desire to love God in a soul, everything is present already; God himself is there, because God is not, nor can he be, anywhere except where there is a desire for his love....

And if this desire of yours is not satisfied, if it seems to you that you always desire without possessing perfect love, all this signifies that you must never say "enough!" It means that we cannot and must not stop on the path of divine love.

To Remain in Christ

Who shall separate us from the love of Christ? Shall tribulation, or distress, or persecution, or famine, or nakedness, or peril, or sword?

—ROMANS 8:35

LAST NIGHT I SPENT THE entire night with Jesus in his passion. I…suffered a great deal…[but] this was a suffering which did me absolutely no harm. My trust in God increased more and more and I felt increasingly attracted towards Jesus…. Although there were no bonds, I felt myself tightly bound to Jesus. I burned with a thousand flames which made me live and die at the same time. Hence, I suffered, lived and died continually…. I would like to shout, to cry out to everyone at the top of my voice: love Jesus….

The Flame of Divine Love

And over all these [virtues] put on love, which binds everything together in perfect harmony.

—COLOSSIANS 3:14

THE HUMAN SPIRIT WITHOUT THE flame of divine love tends to reach the level of the beast, while, on the other hand, charity, the love of God, raises it up so high that it can reach even to the throne of God. Give thanks without ever growing weary for the liberality of such a good Father, and ask him to increase holy charity more and more in your heart.

The Mercy of God

I REMIND YOU OF BALANCE, patience, and sweetness. Quell your excessively vivacious and ardent actions from the outset. I don't know why you are so apprehensive at the trials your soul is sustaining. The soul that fears offending God and has the sincere desire not to do so, but to love him, does not offend him in fact, but loves him. And as this desire is always constant, your every fear is useless and…imaginary.

My daughter, live tranquilly in the presence of God, who has loved you for a long time now, granting you his holy fear….

For pity's sake, I beseech you by all that you hold sacred not to wrong him by entertaining the slightest suspicion that he has abandoned you even for a single moment. This is really one of the most diabolical temptations which you must drive far from you as soon as you are aware of it.

Mercy Amid Misery

Give thanks to the LORD, for he is good,
    for his mercy endures for ever.

—DANIEL 3:67

WHAT AM I TO SAY about my own wretched soul? Alas, it has
been too unfaithful to its Beloved. Praise be to God, however,
who never withdraws his mercy from me.

There are certain moments at which dense clouds appear in
the heavens of my soul, so thick and dark that they do not allow
me to perceive even a feeble ray of light. It is deep night for my
soul. All hell is turned loose upon it with cavernous roars, with
all the evil of its past life, and what is most terrifying is that
my own fantasy and imagination seem determined to conspire
against my soul. The beautiful days spent in the shadow of the
Lord vanish completely from my mind…. This torment does
not last long, nor could it, for if my soul lives through it, this is
only by a remarkable favor from God…. In the midst of such
confusion the apex of my soul is by no means disturbed but
remains extremely tranquil, a fact of which the lower part is
only faintly aware.

Padre Pio's Tact

At that time Jesus went through the grainfields on the sabbath; his disciples were hungry, and they began to pluck heads of grain and to eat. But when the Pharisees saw it, they [rebuked Jesus]…. He said to them…"if you had known what this means, 'I desire mercy, and not sacrifice,' you would not have condemned the guiltless."

—MATTHEW 12:1–3, 7

HIS TACT KNEW NO LIMITS; at the end of one Lent (1923), the friars were astounded to hear—and on Good Friday!—that he wanted a cup of chocolate and fruit, but he knew that one of those present had been indiscreet and over-zealous in fasting during Holy Week and [he added] "Or rather bring two cups of chocolate…one also for this brother tertiary." And because the friars scoffed, [thinking Padre Pio would never break his fast on this day of all days], Padre Pio added, "We will eat together."

St. Pio, thank you for this reminder that true holiness does not come from following rules and regulations of religion, which are so easily mistaken for the essence of faith. Help me aspire to holiness and not settle for looking good.

· TWO ·

A Joyful Spirit

AFTER HE BECAME A FRIAR, his merry-hearted nature helped keep Pio friendly and approachable. But because of his particular vocation and his ascent to sanctity (despite ecstatic prayer moments with God), the passing years brought less and less cause for merriment, humanly speaking. He continued to share witticisms and tell jokes in times of recreation, but his inner life and often-opposed work for souls was serious stuff. His joyful spirit was supernaturally based, existing mysteriously side by side with heavier emotions, including spiritual desolation. It was truly the joy of the Lord.

Yet in the complexity of this great soul, Pio still experienced human joy. Like a child, he lit up when offered some little gift—a piece of candy, perhaps. And in the same way that a mother fighting a terrible illness forgets herself in happiness at her daughter's wedding, Pio looked past his struggles to spiritual fatherhood's joys—whether watching a soul make choices to grow toward holiness or giving Communion to a little girl in a green dress.

A Man Who Laughed

ALL HIS LIFE PADRE PIO was known among his friends as a man with a good sense of humor. Playing pranks on his sisters and fellow novices, and later making his Capuchin brothers laugh by telling innocent little jokes and stories during recreation, Padre Pio fulfilled the paradox that a follower of Christ must both "pick up [his] cross and follow me" and be filled with "the joy of the Lord."

A war story Pio liked to tell was the one of the guileless recruit and the WWI sergeant who was preparing the troops for a visit by the king of Italy. The sergeant knew that the conversation between the king and any given recruit usually followed a formula.

First question: "How old are you?" He practices this with the recruit, who answers, "Twenty-two."

Second question: "How many years have you been in the army?" Again he practices with the recruit to reply, "Two."

Third question: "Whom do you serve more willingly, your king or your country?" To this the recruit is to reply, "Both."

After much practicing with the three questions and their proper answers, the day arrived at last. The king came and inspected the regiment. He began with the questions—but changed the order in which they were asked.

"How many years have you been in the army?" he says.

"Twenty-two," replies the guileless recruit, following the learned response.

"And how old are you?"

"Two."

At this point the sergeant breaks out in a cold sweat as the king frowns and exclaims impatiently, "Either you're stupid or I'm stupid." And the recruit, rejoicing at knowing the right answer replies promptly, "Both, Your Majesty."

Pio's jokes could be made about things like drunkenness too. He would stand up to imitate a drunk trying to hang on to a wall and walk when he told the following: "The drunk saw a millipede walking along a wall and said to God, 'Why, Lord, have you given a thousand feet to this little animal and I can't even hold myself up on two?'"

A Heritage of Joy

PADRE PIO'S FAMILY WAS SO devout, neighbors called them "the family for whom God is everything." But this did not mean they were dour. The trait people most recall about Padre Pio's father, Grazio Forgione, is his joyfulness. A man with a deep love of God, who would walk around an ant, saying, "why should the poor creature die?" Forgione loved to sing with gusto and communicated "a contagious joy."

Padre Pio's mother Giuseppa De Nunzio, who was equally devout, also "knew how to keep merry company." Once her little Francesco (Padre Pio's birth name) upbraided her that her remark "What good looking turnips; I'd like to eat some" as they passed a field might be a sin (in case she was thinking of simply taking one) then asked her to pick him some figs from a tree they passed. "Oh, it's a sin to eat turnips but not a sin to eat figs!" she teased.

Padre Pio's own sense of humor and his love of pranks and jokes was remarked upon by his friends. It cannot be overestimated how important this heritage of joy was to his maintenance of good mental health and freedom from morbidity in his unique apostolate as a spiritual warrior.

True Joys

WHEN HE MOVED INTO ADOLESCENCE, Francesco Forgione did not long for power, riches, sexual conquests, or wild living. Instead, it was the true riches the world offers that drew Franci: to remain with his family, so strong in their love for one another, and to seize the joys he had learned among them. Chief among these was family life itself, with its innocent pleasures of laughter, food, a glass of wine, sharing a good story, praying together, and, above all, knowing they were there for each other in good times and bad.

"Exemplary Novice" Pranks

ON JANUARY 6, 1903, FIFTEEN-YEAR-OLD Francesco Forgione left Pietrelcina with two other boys from his area. His mother, blessing him through her tears, said he belonged now no longer to her but to St. Francis.

After an introductory period of just over two weeks, he began a year of novitiate under a novice master who was severe but also a man "with a heart of gold," full of charity and understanding for the young men he guided. From the beginning, even the strictest Capuchin called Frater Pio [young Capuchins were called Frater, which means "Brother"] "an exemplary novice [who was] an example to all." While gluttony is a common problem to young men, Pio preferred prayer even to eating. Yet he was cheerful and down to earth, retaining his love of pranks and telling jokes when talking was allowed.

One of his pranks took place on a midnight when, as was their habit, the community arose from their beds to pray at a time when many sins take place. Returning from the bathroom with his towel over his shoulder, Pio saw a fellow novice, a very nervous soul who was afraid of his own shadow. The other novice did not notice Pio, who could not resist skulking behind a table, which had on it two candlesticks and a human skull. [2] As the nervous novice crept by the table, Pio groaned and flapped his towel at the boy, who, terrified, fled screaming.

"Wait, it's only me," Pio called, running to silence him before the novice master heard and they got in trouble. Being chased only made the boy scream louder. Finally, Pio caught up to him, just as the boy, in his terror, tripped and fell. Unable to stop in time, Pio tumbled atop the boy, who was so scared that he was too numb to even know where he was. Far from repentant over having so frightened someone, for the rest of his life Pio loved to tell this story.

---

2. Displays like this were common in even American religious houses well into the twentieth century, their purpose being to visually remind onlookers "that thou art dust and unto dust thou shalt return," as a goad to living for eternal joys, not temporal ones.

Tears of Happiness

OH HOW SWEET WAS THE colloquy with paradise that morning! It was such that, although I want to tell you all about it, I cannot. There were things which cannot be translated into human language without losing their deep and heavenly meaning. The heart of Jesus and my own—allow me to use the expression—were fused. No longer were two hearts beating but only one. My own heart had disappeared, as a drop of water is lost in the ocean. Jesus was its paradise, its king. My joy was so intense and deep that I could bear no more, and tears of happiness poured down my cheeks.

Count It All Joy

I SHOULD BE LESS HAPPY if I did not see you so downcast, because I should then see the Lord bestowing less jewels upon you. Hence, in the holy charity of Jesus, while earnestly desiring your spiritual profit and your progress toward perfection, I rejoice more and more to see you in your present state. My joy is by no means foolish, for in the combat there is a crown to be won, and the better the fight put up by the soul, the more numerous the palms of victory.

Don't you know how the apostle St. James exhorted his brethren to rejoice when they were harassed by various storms and numerous reverses? *Count it all joy, my brethren, when you meet various trials* (James 1:2). Moreover, how can we fail to rejoice when we find ourselves involved in many combats, knowing as we do that every victory achieved has a corresponding degree of glory? May the thought of eternal bliss with Jesus and of being made similar to the Son of God encourage you and prevent you from yielding to the enemy's temptations.

The Boy Becomes a Man

For our knowledge is imperfect and our prophecy is imperfect; but when the perfect comes, the imperfect will pass away. When I was a child, I spoke like a child, I thought like a child, I reasoned like a child; when I became a man, I gave up childish ways.

—1 CORINTHIANS 13:9–11

TEASING HIS SISTERS WAS ALWAYS fun. Many times he sneaked up behind two-years-younger Felicita as the little girl washed herself in the portable bathtub on the kitchen floor. With glee the future saint would dunk his little sister's head under the soapy water.

Cheerful under Trial

Count it all joy, my brethren, when you meet various trials, for you know that the testing of your faith produces steadfastness. And let steadfastness have its full effect, that you may be perfect and complete, lacking in nothing.

—JAMES 1:2–4

DURING HIS YEARS AT HOME, struggles between various world powers culminated in the outbreak of World War I in 1914. Italy was swept into the conflict, and the Capuchins, an Order primarily of young men at that time, had many friars and seminarians called up. Pio received his notice—addressed to his birth name of Francesco Forgione.

Such a great ascetic would be expected to shudder at joining the army. Pio *was* distressed but, typically, he worried even more about some of the other friars who had to do military service. Although sad to lay aside his beloved habit, he remained cheerful. He liked Naples and later recalled that during his brief military career there he met many nice people who treated him well.

The Laughter of Happy Men

PADRE AURELIO KNEW PADRE PIO for over fifty years. Between 1916 and 1918, when Aurelio was a seminarian, Padre Pio was the director. Padre Aurelio recalls:

> He...had a fine sense of humor. One day in 1917 we played a practical joke.... We had something like a kite, but it was very, very big. Underneath it we put a little bomb and a little lamp attached to it.... We had a long rope tied to the end of the kite. For about an hour we flew the kite all around the sky. The people saw it and were terrified. Padre Pio and the chief of police knew all about it, but they let us enjoy the joke.

Here is a story someone took down during the friars' recreation period, in which Pio speaks of himself in the third person, then switches to the first, as he tells a tale from his brief military career:

It was his turn to go somewhere.... Our soldier courageously armed himself with an umbrella and, well protected, he went on his way along Piazza Plebiscito [in Naples].

"Hey, soldier," but the soldier went straight on as if he hadn't heard anything.

"Hey, I'm talking to you, soldier." It was a Colonel who, justifiably, was becoming impatient. He had to turn back.

"What kind of thing is this?" roared the Colonel under the rain that was drenching him. "A soldier with an umbrella! Have you gone crazy?"

I offered him my umbrella [saying] ,"If the Colonel wants to protect himself, I will accompany him…."

The Colonel realized he was dealing with a dull recruit and with a gesture of annoyance, turned away from me and left me there with my umbrella in my hand.

The Satisfactions of Spiritual Parenthood

PADRE PIO, THOSE WHO LIVED with him testify, year after year lived in aridity and darkness, a warrior battling unceasingly for souls, while never sure whether he himself was pleasing God. At the same time he received great satisfaction, even joy, from the spiritual progress of his spiritual children—a joy that itself was purely supernatural, not an overflow of a constant state of mirth and contentment. He writes to one:

> As regards your spiritual state, I exhort you in the most sweet Lord to live tranquilly. I have a great reason to praise the Lord, for having enlightened your spirit somewhat.
>
> Knowing that you are always resigned to the will of heaven fills my soul with superlative joy.

"A Human Being Like Everybody Else"

ANDRE MANDATO, AN AMERICAN FROM New Jersey testified: [When I first started visiting Padre Pio] there wasn't much of a crowd, because it was hard for the people to get there. We could go into the little garden, where there were maybe ten people, and we visited with him. He was jovial, in good humor. He told jokes. When you were by yourself, you would say: "he is a saint." But when he talked with you, you didn't see the saint. You saw a human being like everybody else, smiling, joking. I could touch him. I'd talk with him just [as I'd talk with anyone else].

Peace

PEACE IS SIMPLICITY OF HEART, serenity of mind, tranquility of soul, the bond of love. Peace means order, harmony in our whole being; it means continual contentment springing from the knowledge of a good conscience; it is the holy joy of a heart in which God reigns. Peace is the way to perfection, indeed in peace is perfection to be found. The devil, who is well aware of all this, makes every effort to have us lose our peace.

Joy to All of Good Will

LIVE JOYFULLY AND COURAGEOUSLY, AT least in the upper part of the soul, amid the trials in which the Lord places you. Live joyfully and courageously, I repeat, because the angel who foretells the birth of our little Savior and Lord...sings, announcing that he brings tidings of joy, peace, and happiness to men of good will. So...there is nobody who does not know that in order to receive this Child, it is sufficient to be of good will.... He came to bless good will, which little by little he will render fruitful and effective, as long as we allow ourselves to be governed by it. And I hope that we...will do so.

Be Joyful!

I will greatly rejoice in the LORD,
my soul shall exult in my God.

—ISAIAH 61:10

PADRE PIO WAS NOT ONE who usually counseled rejoicing and joy in his spiritual directives, but he certainly lived it, as the friars who shared his life have attested. His speech was salted with witticisms, never unkind but truly funny. At recreation, whether with other friars or with his many lay friends, Padre Pio was a joyous man.

Lord, you called Padre Pio to do spiritual battle from the time he was a teenager until almost his last hour, helping you snatch souls from darkness and death. Yet he kept a joyful spirit, laughed often, and brought this joy and laughter to his friends and confreres. May I, too, laugh much and carry your joy with me wherever I go.

Let's Laugh

For everything there is a season and a time for every matter under heaven:

…

a time to weep, and a time to laugh.

—ECCLESIASTES 3:1, 4

I LAUGH AT YOUR SUFFERING, as you, many times, laughed at mine…. If you can, laugh at yourself with me, and pray that I too can laugh at myself with you.

Yes, Lord, help me not to take myself too seriously but to laugh readily at myself. Even my worst troubles have a ridiculous side.

Specks and Logs

Why do you see the speck that is in your brother's eye, but do not notice the log that is in your own eye?

—LUKE 6:41

I CANNOT TOLERATE CRITICISM AND speaking ill of our brothers. It is true, sometimes I enjoy teasing them, but speaking ill of them makes me sick. We have so many defects in ourselves to criticize, why pick on our brothers? And lacking in charity we damage the roots of the tree of life, with the risk of killing it.

A Beautiful Heart Trumps Fine Dress

ANNA MARIA D'ORAZI WAS A young boarding school student when she came with her mother to visit Padre Pio shortly after World War II. It was May 5, a day at San Giovanni Rotondo when Padre Pio presided over children's First Communions. Maria had not yet made her First Communion because her mother, a dress designer, had not yet found time to make a splendid white dress and organize the traditional party. Now Anna Maria experienced a burning desire to make her First Communion this day.

Her mother disapproved, saying she would be like an orphan with no party, no presents, and no dress. Finally she told her child to ask Padre Pio, thinking he would say no. But when Anna Maria asked the Padre after he heard her confession, he agreed that the absence of the white dress meant nothing.

However, the world did not agree with Anna Maria and Padre Pio. When the children were lined up, Anna Maria, in her simple green dress, was not allowed to go with the other girls, who looked like little brides in their white dresses. She was pushed aside until the last of the boys, also dressed in their smartest, had received Jesus. Finally, last of all, she was permitted to kneel at the communion rail.

Anna Maria recalls, "I saw Padre Pio coming toward me, radiant and smiling, while he held the Sacred Host in his fingers above the ciborium, and when he was directly in front of me I heard him say: 'Get up and come here.' I got up and followed him.... He made me climb the altar steps, and he gave me Communion in front of the tabernacle. A hushed murmur of voices filled the whole church, everyone...greatly moved.... All this was explained to me afterward by my mother, more moved and overwhelmed than myself, because I did not understand the significance of Padre Pio's gesture. I was only enraptured...because I was making my First Communion.... The sweetness of this memory accompanies me in the most difficult moments in my life."

Laughing at Myself

A cheerful heart is a good medicine.

—PROVERBS 17:22

WHILE HE ENDURED CONSTANT PAIN from his stigmata and, in his latter years, other ailments, Padre Pio was known for enjoying a hearty laugh. Besides his true spiritual children, there were "followers" of Padre Pio who let superstition creep into devotion to him. While he found this annoying and sometimes even got angry when it went too far, in general he maintained a healthy, humorous perspective.

An example: Some of these devotees would call out as he passed, "Padre Pio, my mother had cancer, and I put your picture on her chest, and it disappeared." "Padre Pio, my child was very sick, and I put your picture on him, and he got immediately well." Padre Pio heard so much of the efficacy of his picture and was pretty tired of what he considered rank superstition.

One night, praying alone very late in the choir of the church, he heard footsteps back and forth in the silence of the night. Eventually this disturbed his prayer. He got up and looked out the window. He saw a sinister-looking figure in a cape with something in his hand that might [have been] a grenade or bomb.

This was a time of great political unrest, and Padre Alessio Parente later recalled Pio's telling the other friars, "At first I was so scared he would throw the bomb at me. But then I said to myself, 'Oh, don't worry; I think I've got a picture of Padre Pio somewhere.'"

Lord, help me to always laugh and, above all, laugh at myself in situations where pretentiousness or pride could arise.

Testimonies

THE FRIARY OF OUR LADY of Grace publishes a magazine which features letters detailing graces received through the prayer intercession of the dead saint. Here are some samples:

* * *

I suffered from severe depression, diagnosed as manic. My family was all deeply upset as it was pronounced to be incurable. During my last visit to a hospital in 1976 a patient placed the little leaflet with the third class relic on it in my hand. I said the prayer then and there although I did not know anything about Padre Pio. I have never since suffered from depression.

* * *

[On] Christmas Eve, my car died. It was really hard for me as a single parent of three not having a car.... I couldn't afford a loan for a car so I prayed to the Lord, along with the prayers for Padre Pio's intercession.... One of my sisters said to be specific in prayer...so I prayed for a dependable car. (I liked little red sports cars with black interiors).... Anyway this past Christmas I ran into a friend...[who] signed [her extra] car over to me in January. Praise God, it is a dependable car, but also a red car with black interior. We laugh but I know the dear Padre helped me.

A Little Flower

PADRE GERARDO OF DELICETO, WHO lived with Pio, wrote: The sixteenth of October was the anniversary of my feast day. As always, I had gone to the office to work. I had not seen the Padre and therefore waited impatiently for 11 o'clock to greet him. That morning I [didn't] hear his rhythmic and dragging footsteps accompanied by loud coughs.

I carried on with my work when, suddenly, it seemed to me that someone had stopped at my door and touched it delicately. Suspicious, I got up and opened the door. It was he, smiling and a bit embarrassed, like a child surprised by his mother while playing some trick.

"Good wishes," he said to me, and gave me a little flower that he had put in the keyhole.

About His Gruffness

ONE DAY I WAS WITH Padre Pio near the sacristy. It was jam-packed, and we couldn't get through with the wheelchair. I [and another Capuchin were] trying to push our way through the crowd. We were shouting, but the people would not cooperate.

Padre Pio too was shouting: "Let me through!"

Finally when we did get through the crowd, he said: "Don't worry. I didn't get angry in my soul. I was shouting, but my heart was laughing."

The only time some people respected him was when he shouted at them. He told me: "I'll never get angry inside myself. If I ever get angry inside, it won't be for this reason."

The same applies to his roughness in the confessional—it was only to make people live a good life. His harsh words, his shouting, were something that changed people. They would tell me that they had been away from God for forty, fifty, or sixty years. When Padre Pio shouted at them, it was the shock or jolt they needed to come back to God.

· THREE ·

Healing, Signs, and Miracles

JESUS WORKED MIRACLES OF MANY kinds and urged people to believe because of these works, if they could believe in him for no other reason (see John 10:3). For that reason—to be a sign of supernatural realities inviting us to God—inexplicable signs, healings, and other miracles occur in every era through at least some saints. Pio's life is rich in all three.

He received signs to guide him, physical miracles such as the imposition of the stigmata, and bodily healings. His prayers and offered sufferings obtained graces of every kind for others: from the vanquishing of crop-ravaging insects to belief given to atheists or a car able to run on empty.

Gifted, among many other charisms, with that of healing, Pio brought God's miracle cures to sufferers of cancer, blindness, deafness, injuries, heart disease, and many other illnesses, including sicknesses of the soul and mind, such as hatred, violence, or depression. These healings have continued after his death when his prayers are asked.

May we see all these works of God through Pio for what they are: consoling reminders of God's and Pio's love for the human family—and for each of us.

Testing the Mystic's Authenticity

BEGINNING IN EARLY 1912 WHEN Padre Pio was living in his native Pietrelcina for health reasons, one of Padre Pio's two spiritual directors, Padre Agostino of San Marco in Lamis, decided to test the authenticity of Padre Pio's sanctity. He did this by writing to him in French and Greek, languages Padre Pio did not know. Padre Pio had no problem receiving letters even in Greek. He had his Guardian Angel translate them for him.

Authenticity for this is found in a statement appended to the end of one of these letters. Dated August 25, 1919, it is written by the parish priest Salvatore Pannullo. Pannullo writes: "I, the undersigned, testify under oath that when Padre Pio received this letter, he explained its contents to me literally. When I asked him how he could read and explain it, as he did not know even the Greek alphabet, he replied: 'You know, my Guardian Angel explained it all to me.'"

Inexplicable Signs

YESTERDAY EVENING SOMETHING HAPPENED TO me which I can neither explain nor understand. In the center of the palms of my hands a red patch appeared, about the size of a cent and accompanied by acute pain. The pain was much more acute in the left hand and it still persists. I also feel some pain in the soles of my feet.

This phenomenon has been repeated several times for almost a year now, but for some time past it had not occurred. Do not be disturbed by the fact that this is the first time I have mentioned it, for I was invariably overcome by abominable shame. If you only knew what it costs me to tell you about it now! I have lots of things to tell you but find no words. I can only say that when I am close to Jesus in the Blessed Sacrament, my heart throbs so violently that it seems to me at times that it must burst out of my chest.

Sometimes at the altar my whole body burns in an indescribable manner. My face in particular seems to go on fire. I have no idea, dear Father, what these signs mean.

"*My Crucifixion*"

ON THE MORNING OF THE 20ᵗʰ of last month [in 1918], in the choir, after I had celebrated Mass, I yielded to a sweet sleep [in fact, this was an ecstasy]. All the internal and external senses and even the very faculties of my soul were immersed in indescribable stillness. Absolute silence surrounded and invaded me. I was suddenly filled with great peace and abandonment which effaced everything else and caused a lull in the [spiritual] turmoil [of the dark night in which he lived spiritually]. All this happened in a flash.

While this was taking place I saw before me a mysterious person similar to the one I had seen on the evening of 5 August. The only difference was that his hands and feet and side were dripping blood. The sight terrified me and what I felt at that moment is indescribable. I thought I should die and really should have died if the Lord had not intervened and strengthened my heart which was about to burst out of my chest.

The vision disappeared and I became aware that my hands, feet and side were dripping blood. Imagine the agony I experienced and continue to experience almost every day. The heart wound bleeds continually, especially from Thursday evening until Saturday. Dear father, I am dying of pain because of the wounds and the resulting embarrassment I feel deep in my soul. I'm afraid I shall bleed to death if the Lord does not hear my heartfelt supplication to relieve me of this condition....

...After Pio told him what had happened...[Padre] Benedetto [one of Pio's spiritual directors]...wrote Pio's second director Padre Agostino the following: "The signs on him are neither stains nor marks, but real wounds which perforate his hands and feet. I have [also] observed the wound in his side, a veritable gash which exudes blood or a bloody humor. On Fridays it's blood. When I saw him for the first time he was barely able to stand on his feet, but when I took my leave of him he was able to celebrate Mass.... When he celebrates Mass, the 'gifts' are exposed to the public as he has to raise his bare hands."

Keeping It Quiet

IN NAPLES, THE OWNER OF the secular newspaper heard about Pio's stigmata and commissioned an outstanding writer...to travel to Our Lady of Grace and investigate. What was going on in this friary? Chicanery? Dark Age superstition with no foundation in reality? Or something genuine?

Padre Paolino [the friary guardian] had strict orders to keep quiet. But the naïve Franciscan did not believe this meant he must lie if asked direct questions or refuse Franciscan hospitality to anyone. At that time there were no inns or hotels in San Giovanni. A crowd simply camped out among the goats and sheep as they waited to attend Padre Pio's Mass, have him hear their confessions, and pray over their sick. When the noted journalist arrived among them, he asked Paolino to introduce him to Pio. Paolino did so, and Pio, who had no idea who this person was, chatted with the journalist about Naples, for which Pio expressed fond memories from his army days. The journalist observed Pio's simplicity, his down-to-earth warmth, and his loving-kindness to all who came to him. The writer was impressed that before him was not a charlatan but a man truly trying to live up to the ideals of St. Francis.

Then a miracle happened in front of the journalist's world-weary eyes. A young man on crutches was told by Padre Pio to drop them and walk.

The man had no faith and protested, "I'll fall." At last, urged on by Pio, he dropped the crutches, but clutched fearfully at the wall to support himself.

"Come on, walk." Pio laughed. Something in that confident laugh caught the crippled man's soul. He let go of the wall. He walked. His foot, mangled in an accident, had been healed.

The journalist interviewed the young man, a cultured fellow whose doctors had agreed the foot required surgery if he were ever to hope to walk again. The young man had come not for himself but for his polio-crippled child.... After the father's healing, he went back on behalf of his child and was told to keep praying for the child's cure, too.

The article about all this was a sensation, especially because it appeared in a secular newspaper written by a well-known intellectual who had no axe to grind on behalf of Christianity or the Catholic Church.

God's Healing through His Saints

NOT LONG AFTER WORLD WAR II a Polish woman physician, a survivor of a Nazi concentration camp, came down with terminal cancer. Her friend Cardinal Wojtyla in Rome sent a message to Padre Pio, to whom he had once confessed on a visit to San Giovanni Rotondo. Padre Pio, receiving the little note, remarked, "I cannot say no to this."

Shortly thereafter, the doctors decided they had been mistaken. The woman was not terminal: It was an inflammation, not a cancerous growth. Wanda Poltawska went on with her life as a mother, wife, and doctor. She knew nothing of her friend's intervention nor of Padre Pio. Even when she eventually learned of the Cardinal's letter and his subsequent one of thanks, she says she didn't want to reflect on what might have happened. But in 1967 she had an opportunity to go to Rome and that May went to San Giovanni Rotondo. She attended Padre Pio's Mass and later wrote, "It is impossible to find adequate words to describe this Mass."

After [the Mass], on his way to [the] sacristy, [Pio] stopped, looked about him, and then found Wanda in the crowd. She says: "I shall never forget his glance. Smiling, he came even closer to me, patted me on the head, and said, 'Adesso, va bene?'

('Now you are OK?') I did not answer; I had no time. What could I say? But…I knew he recognized me. In this moment I also knew that it wasn't because of a wrong diagnosis that I had found myself suddenly well several years earlier."

The Odor of Sanctity

AMONG THE ACCUSATIONS DURING THE first decade after Padre Pio received the visible stigmata was that he—most unsuitably for a friar—used perfume. In time it became understood that what people sometimes—not always—smelled around Pio was not something from a bottle: it was instead often an odor emanating from his blood. Dr. Giorgio Festa, who wrote extensively from firsthand study on the stigmata of Padre Pio, once took cloths saturated with blood from Pio's stigmata wounds with him when he drove back to Rome. Blood rapidly becomes putrid with a foul odor but for a long time these cloths gave off a wonderful perfume that filled not only the car Festa drove but also the office in Rome where they were stored.

Naturally inexplicable perfumes also seemed to indicate the unseen presence of Padre Pio among his many spiritual children by the phenomena of bilocation. One of Pio's converts, for instance, after meeting the stigmatic, adopted the habit of beginning work at his typewriter with the sign of the cross. One day when he forgot, he immediately smelled an odor for which he could find no natural cause. He recognized it as a smell connected to Pio and told his family, most of whom smelled it too, that the Padre had "come" to give him a friendly reminder not to forget to pray when he started to work.

This phenomenon, known as the odor of sanctity, was not, in Pio's case, always the same. Some people, even at the same moment, smelled a flowery perfume, others smelled incense, others "fine tobacco," and still others nothing. Whatever the odor, it always heralded some grace given through the prayer intercession of Padre Pio. A nun, for instance, who had written the overwhelmed stigmatic priest twice about some concerns without receiving an answer, woke one night to this odor. She immediately sensed that Pio was there in some way, assuring her that he had taken her prayer requests to heart. From that moment, she felt herself borne along on a great current of peace—a grace much more important than the perfume that had signaled it.

Years later, after his death, testimonies of favors and graces received by people who asked Padre Pio's prayer intercession would sometimes mention wonderful perfumes that had no possible human source.

Pio Predicts Future Events by Divine Inspiration

PADRE CARMELO DURANTE WITNESSED VARIOUS examples of Padre Pio's gift of prophecy. Carmelo testified:

> During the last world war, I would spend the summer holidays from the Gregorian Pontifical University of Rome—where I was studying—at San Giovanni Rotondo close to my spiritual director Padre Pio.
>
> It was the summer of 1942. Naturally we spoke about the war every day and particularly of the resounding military victories of Germany on all the battlefronts....
>
> Italy and Germany were allies; but [then Italy made peace with England and America and then declared war on her former ally, Germany].
>
> [One] day in the friary hallway Padre Pio said to me, "Italy will lose the war out of the mercy of God, not because of his justice."
>
> And I appealed..."But Padre, how can one lose a war out of mercy and not out of justice?"

He responded..."Yes, it is as I say, Italy will lose the war out of the mercy of God, because if she won the war with Germany, the war over, Germany would crush Italy under its feet." And he stamped his foot on the ground with force to bring across what that meant.

Later it became clear to me how losing the war for Italy was really a victory and not a disgrace at all, but a grace.

A Far-Traveling Man

FOR ROUGHLY FIFTY YEARS PADRE Pio was unable to leave the friary, lest the local people take arms to keep him there. Yet, he continued to appear at various places around the world.... The only son of a lawyer and a schoolteacher...was fighting in Libya as a lieutenant during the terrible Battle of Tobruk [1942]. Seriously wounded but conscious, he became aware that a line of English tanks WAS moving toward where he lay, unable to move. When one of the armored vehicles was only a few meters away from flattening him, a chaplain dragged the lieutenant to safety.

The young man survived and eventually returned to Italy. He never forgot the chaplain, however, and always longed to be able to thank him. One day he found his devout mother reading a book and there was a photo of the priest who had saved him. It was Padre Pio.

Obtaining leave, he traveled to Our Lady of Grace, but when he saw Padre Pio surrounded by so many people, he became shy. He said to himself he would come back another time when he had a longer leave and speak to Padre Pio then. But as he prepared to leave, Pio called across the sacristy,

"Mario,…now that you have found me you are leaving without saying 'hello'?"

The crowd parted to let the dazed young man through. With a few words encouraging him to practice his religion, Padre Pio hugged the young man whose life he had saved. That was the start of a long relationship, with many trips by the lawyer's son to San Giovanni Rotondo.

Two Places at Once

A TESTIMONY FROM PADRE ALBERTO:

One afternoon in May 1928, I saw Padre Pio near the window, staring out, his gaze fixed. He seemed absorbed. I drew near to kiss his hand, but I had the sensation that his hand was stiff. At the same moment, I heard him pronounce the words of absolution in a very clear voice.

Immediately I ran to call Father Tomaso, the superior. The two of us approached Padre Pio, who was pronouncing the last words of absolution. At that Padre Pio gave a jerk as if he had come back out of drowsiness. He turned to us and said: "You're here? I didn't realize you were here."

A few days later a telegram arrived at the friary from a city in northern Italy. The telegram thanked the father superior for having sent Padre Pio to assist a dying man. From the telegram we understood that the man was dying at the exact moment Padre Pio was pronouncing the words of absolution.

The Vast Spiritual World

And as soon as I have gone from you, the Spirit of the LORD
will carry you I know not where.

—1 KINGS 18:12

NO THANKS ARE DUE TO me for the visit which the Lord
allowed me to pay you in spirit, so let your thanks and praise
be directed to God alone. You ask me to tell you the day and
the hour of this visit. I am very reluctant to reveal this to you,
but as I don't want to distress you, I'll stifle the repugnance I
feel. If I am not mistaken, a visit of this kind took place on 4
October [1914], the feast of our Seraphic Father, St. Francis,
and in the early hours of the following day.

I cannot tell you any more about that visit. I can only tell
you that it was quite a long one. I beseech you not to say a
word about it to a living soul on this earth. In fact, I don't deny
that I should very much like you to burn this letter as well as
mine of the tenth. What do you say to that? Will my desire be
satisfied? However, do as you please in this, for I wouldn't wish
to trouble you in the slightest way. Whatever you decide to do
in this matter, will you please be so good as to let me know.

Bilocation: Sent as God's Messenger

SR. MARIA GELTRUDE OF THE Sacred Heart of Jesus was a Capuchin nun in the Convent of San Giovanni Battista at Bagnacavallo. A great woman of prayer, God permitted her some terrible temptations as well as incredible graces. During a period of the terrible temptations, a fellow Capuchin, a priest, advised her to seek help from Padre Pio. She did not believe he could do anything for her, but she prayed and asked the archangel St. Raphael to intercede for her.

On January 20, 1950, she had the shock of seeing in her cell Padre Pio. Standing by the window, he upbraided her severely for her discouragement. Sr. Geltrude began to weep, and Padre Pio sat down, the nun on her knees at his feet. Now he spoke to her in a fatherly way and put his hands on her head. At his touch, the temptations left her completely, never to return.

The Wife Beater

Then Philip opened his mouth, and beginning with this scripture he told him the good news of Jesus. And as they went along the road they came to some water, and the eunuch said, "See, here is water! What is to prevent my being baptized?" And Philip said, "If you believe with all your heart, you may." And he replied, "I believe that Jesus Christ is the Son of God." And he commanded the chariot to stop, and they both went down into the water, Philip and the eunuch, and he baptized him. And when they came up out of the water, the Spirit of the Lord caught up Philip; and the eunuch saw him no more, and went on his way rejoicing. But Philip was found at Azotus, and passing on he preached the gospel to all the towns till he came to Caesarea.

—Acts 8:35–40

Giovanni, a taxi driver and Communist, used to get drunk and beat his wife. One night he had done precisely that and then threw himself on the bed. When he hit it he felt somebody shake it violently. He looked towards the end of the bed and, to his amazement, saw a Capuchin friar giving him an icy stare. The friar told him in no uncertain terms what he thought of his behavior and then he seemed to disappear. Giovanni jumped up from the bed, and [found only his wife in the house]. The poor lady denied all knowledge of any friar, but her husband wouldn't believe her.

The poor woman [who] had prayed at length to Padre Pio [requesting his intercession] had heard of his powers of bilocation. There could be no other explanation for it: Padre Pio had come to help her! [Hearing this,] Giovanni was angry [and] decided to go have "a look" at this friar.

Giovanni [went] to San Giovanni, Rotondo. He found Padre Pio, recognized him, and spoke to him. To make a long story short, the convinced Communist, wife beater, and drunk was converted to Christ.

Miracle on a Bus

ENNIO ROSSI REMEMBERS A DAY during the summer of 1947: In order to please my wife we went to San Giovanni Rotondo to see Padre Pio. [But] we were told that Padre Pio was ill and that it was impossible to see him. That is how we found ourselves chatting [on a homeward-bound bus] with a distinguished-looking man and a young boy.

The man told us his son had become completely deaf, and the best specialists to whom he had taken him had given no hope of recovery. So he had come to Padre Pio to ask for his powerful intercession with our Lord, and he had been accompanied to Padre Pio's cell, where his son received his blessing with the promise: "Go in peace, I will pray for you."

The young boy was looking out of the window at the countryside. Suddenly he turned to his father and said loudly: "But why are you shouting so?" And surprised to see that we were talking quietly, he immediately realized he was cured and exclaimed delightedly, "Daddy, I can hear! Daddy, I can hear!"

A Miracle for the Miracle Worker

IN 1959, EXHAUSTED FROM FORTY years of bearing the stigmata while laboring incessantly to bring souls to God, Padre Pio was hospitalized in the Home for the Relief of Suffering. Serious pleurisy necessitated extracting pleural liquid a number of times. Padre Pio begged [for permission to leave] the hospital so he could die in the friary. This was granted and Pio returned to the friary July 3. On August 5, while he was still ill, the statue of Our Lady of Fatima, which was on pilgrimage in the area, was brought to San Giovanni Rotondo.

...The next day shortly before the statue took its leave, Pio had himself carried down on a chair...during the "farewell" Mass. After Mass the statue was carried into the old sacristy and Padre Pio bowed his head, with his ever-ready tears of devotion. He kissed the statue of Mary—she who had appeared to him so many times—and put a rosary he had blessed in the statue's hands. Carried back to his cell, he was so exhausted it was feared he would collapse....

Testimony of what next took place before a helicopter arrived to take the statue on to its next stop is from the account of eyewitness Father Raffaele of S. Elia a Pianisi:

Padre Pio expressed the desire to salute the Madonna once again…and so he was brought into the choir of the new church on a chair once again and he looked out of the last window to the right…. Amidst the shouts of the masses, "Viva! Viva!" the helicopter rose…but before taking its course, it circled the friary and church three times in order to say good-bye to Padre Pio.

And he, on seeing the helicopter take its leave with the Madonna on board said: "Madonna, my mother, you came to Italy and found me ailing; and now you depart leaving me ill." Having said this he bowed his head, while he shuddered from head to foot. Padre Pio obtained the grace he asked for and he now feels well….

In the meantime, however, Professor Gasbarrini [M.D.] arrived providentially; he meticulously examined Padre Pio and found him clinically cured. Thus he told all those priests present, and I am among them: "Padre Pio is well and he can celebrate Mass in the church tomorrow."

The Resurrection Life Begins

SHORTLY BEFORE PADRE PIO DIED...the stigmata he had borne for fifty years showed their first change. The father guardian at that time notes in the friary chronicles that "they gradually began to close, and the bleeding diminished, until they appeared at his death completely healed and without any scars."

In what was another miracle, Dr. Giuseppe Sala writes:

> Ten minutes after his death, Padre Pio's hands, thorax, and feet were held up by me...and were photographed by a friar in the presence of four other confreres. The hands, feet, [and] thorax...showed no signs of wounds; nor were scars present on [any]... areas where during his life, he had well-defined and visible wounds. The skin on the above-mentioned areas was the same as that on the rest of his body: soft, elastic, and mobile.... These wounds which Padre Pio had had during his life, and which disappeared on his death, must be considered to be a fact beyond all clinical behavior and of a supernatural nature.

A Healing Mystery: Relics

DURING THE LIFETIME OF PADRE Pio the Lord healed many sick, even terminally ill, people through the prayers or appearances of Padre Pio, sometimes through bilocation. Since his death, many people have been healed through asking his prayer intercession with God while touching something that Pio once wore or used, such as the bandages from his stigmata or a piece of his Franciscan habit. [Such items are called relics.] A typical testimony:

> I have a nephew who was born blind. The doctors said he would never see. I asked Fr. Fanning if I might have one of Padre Pio's relics for a short time. He lent it to me, and I applied it to the baby's eyes. In about two weeks we noticed that he was following objects. His parents took him to the eye specialist, who said the child could see, but he had no medical explanation for why.

Lord, I thank you that you have given and are giving so many miracles of your healing through St. Pio. You have certainly kept your promise that your disciples would do the same works you did on earth. Padre Pio, pray for all us who need physical healing!

The Case of Agnes Stump

TWENTY YEARS OLD, AGNES HAD never had even a headache; now after a year of a pain in her left knee, an x-ray diagnosed a tumor. Her father and brother visited Padre Pio, who advised surgery, adding, "I will guide the surgeon's hand." On January 2, 1968, surgery was done and healing progressed well until October, a month after Pio's death, when the cancer spread once more. On October 14, 1968, new surgery with tissue biopsied in three institutes revealed "sarcomatosis growth of the mieloplasma tumor." Amputation was advised. A second specialist said amputation wasn't necessary but he advised more surgery to stiffen the leg, which she refused. A third specialist wanted to operate at once.

Agnes visited the tomb of Padre Pio that December 20. Without any of the recommended surgeries but only application of a relic [a blood-stained bandage from the Padre's side wound], Agnes awaited God's help. On April 25, 1969, Padre Pio having come to her shortly before in a beautiful dream, she suddenly began to walk without crutches. Tests showed the disease had stopped spreading. After two years of almost complete immobility, Agnes walked to Padre Pio's tomb in September 1969, kneeling there completely cured.

God's Healing Power
through His Saints

IN 1974 I WAS THE recipient of what my husband and I consider a miracle from Padre Pio. I was told in July 1974 [that] I would be opened up for major cancer. Since I was also a nurse at the hospital, I knew the score. The surgeon told me quite bluntly: "We are opening you up for major cancer, with the expectation of finding it, and praying we don't."

The night before surgery my husband awakened about 2:00 a.m. to the scent of roses (a miracle in itself since he was just out of the hospital from nose surgery and could smell nothing at all). He followed the scent to the living room, where on the mantel was a continuous candle burning in front of a statue of Padre Pio. Suddenly he heard a voice, and it said, "Rudolph, don't worry; they won't find cancer: she'll be all right." My husband was stunned.

The next morning I was in surgery six hours. Then the doctor came into my room smiling and said to me, "Do you know you had a miracle? There isn't a trace of cancer in your body anywhere. A large tumor was removed, and it was benign."

· FOUR ·

Prayer

"A SIMPLE FRIAR WHO PRAYS," Pio described himself. It would have been unthinkable for him to say, "who prays with power." Yet anyone familiar with the fruits of Pio's prayers—such as the regional hospital across the street from the friary—has to be awed at the brown-clad Capuchin's humility.

That he described himself only in terms of one who prays should not be taken as simple humility, however. Prayer was the foundation and main work of Pio's life. He prayed in everything he did. Prayer *powered* everything he did. In prayer, Pio gained access to God. Early on, he sometimes saw Jesus and dialogued with him. Later in Pio's spiritual maturity, Jesus hid himself in the game of love, safeguarding Pio's humility, leaving him uncertain of Jesus's approval. Far from giving up prayer, Pio prayed all the more.

Out of these selfless prayers sent into the silent darkness not only came God's miracles, including transformed lives, but—sticking with God when it was hard as well as when it was sweet—Pio was himself transformed into a saint.

Prayer

PRAYER IS THE OXYGEN OF the soul!

A remark of the Padre's in passing, according to the Padre's spiritual son Father Joseph Pius Martin of Our Lady of Grace Friary, San Giovanni Rotondo, who lived with and assisted him in his later years.

Cry Aloud to God

[WHEN YOUR] TRIAL IS VERY hard, I repeat for the umpteenth time that you are not to be afraid, for Jesus is with you even when you see your soul, as it were, on the brink of the precipice. You must invariably lift up your voice to heaven even when desolation invades your soul. Cry aloud along with that most patient man, Job, who when the Lord placed him in the state which you are now experiencing, cried out to him: "Even if you slay me Lord, I will still hope in you" [Job 13:15].

The Holy Spirit Guides His Prayer

YOU COMPLAIN THAT I DON'T answer all your questions and chide me gently on this account. All I can do is ask your pardon and beg you not to be angry with me, for I am not to blame. For some time past I have been suffering from forgetfulness, despite all my good intentions to satisfy every demand made on me. I am told [by my spiritual director] that this is a very special grace of the heavenly Father.

The Lord only allows me to recall those persons and things he wants me to remember. In point of fact, on several occasions our merciful Lord has suggested to me people whom I have never known or even heard of, for the sole purpose of having me present them to him and intercede for them, [whereupon] he never fails to answer my poor feeble prayers. On the other hand, when Jesus doesn't want to answer me, he makes me actually forget to pray for those persons for whom I had firmly decided and intended to pray.

Daily Prayer

I will meditate on your precepts,
　and fix my eyes on your ways.

—Psalm 119:15

As regards...meditation, I exhort you to establish at least two periods a day for this purpose. Try to spend not less than half an hour for each period. Try to see that those periods of meditation are possibly in the morning, in order to prepare yourself for the battle, and in the evening, in order to purify your soul from any earthly affections which have become attached to it during the day. Try to take up once again the practice of the holy hour [prayer before the Blessed Sacrament], which you used to do before—always, however, within the limits of possibility, without causing yourself serious discomfort.

Lord, help me to pray regularly and before I begin each day. Help me also to more regularly spend a little time with you before bed.

Padre Pio on the Rosary

Love our Lady and make her loved; always recite the rosary
and recite it as often as possible. [To comments that the
rosary had had its day] Let's do what we have always done;
that which our fathers always did and we will be fine…. Satan
always tries to destroy this prayer, but he will never succeed. It
is the prayer of He who triumphs over all and everyone. And
she has taught us this prayer just as Jesus taught us the Our
Father.

When someone asked whether one should pay attention to
the words of the Hail Mary (i.e., vocal prayer or to the mental
contemplation of the mysteries of the rosary), he replied:

The attention must be on the "Hail Mary" and to the greet-
ings which you give to the Virgin and on the mysteries which
you contemplate. She is present in all the mysteries and she
participated in everything with love and pain.

In Padre Pio's letter dated May 13, 1915, to the Franciscan
tertiary Raffaelina Cerase:

Reflect upon and keep before your mental gaze the
great humility of the Mother of God, our Mother.
The more she was filled with heavenly gifts, the more

deeply did she humble herself, so that she was able to say when overshadowed by the Holy Spirit, who made her the Mother of God's Son, "Behold the Handmaid of the Lord." This dear Mother of ours was to break forth with the same words in the home of St. Elizabeth, although she bore in her chaste womb the Word Incarnate.

Prayer, Always Prayer

CAPUCHIN EUSEBIO NOTTE WITNESSES:

One evening when we were in his cell…the discussion turned to the Rosary. To provoke Padre Pio into telling me how many rosaries he had said that day [I told him I had said three rosaries of five decades and said, "How about you? Forty?" To which Pio replied,] "I have said sixty of fifteen decades but keep it to yourself!"

On that day alone he had said 60 complete rosaries, which means 180 of those we usually say…. [Then] you think that he carried out that activity which we all know…hours of meditation, three or four hours of confessions, many hours for Mass, with preparation and thanksgiving, people who continually besieged him…and so on—then we are astounded and wonder how this man managed to say so many prayers. This is a question for which I have never found an answer!

Wait Tranquilly for Heaven's Dew

ANXIETY IS ONE OF THE greatest traitors that real virtue and solid devotion [to God] can ever have. It pretends to warm us to do good works, but doesn't and we grow cold; it makes us run only to make us trip. One must be careful of this on all occasions, particularly at prayer. And to better succeed it would be well to remember that graces and consolations of prayer are not waters of this earth, but of Heaven. Therefore all our efforts are not sufficient to make them fall, even though it is necessary to prepare oneself with great diligence but always humbly and tranquilly. One must keep one's heart turned toward Heaven and wait from there the heavenly dew.

Calm in the Storm

One day he got into a boat with his disciples, and he said to them, "Let us go across to the other side of the lake." So they put out, and while they were sailing he fell asleep. A windstorm swept down on the lake, and the boat was filling with water, and they were in danger. They went to him and woke him up, shouting, "Master, Master, we are perishing!" And he woke up and rebuked the wind and the raging waves; they ceased, and there was a calm. He said to them, "Where is your faith?" They were afraid and amazed, and said to one another, "Who then is this, that he commands even the winds and the water, and they obey him?"

—Luke 8:22–25

How important it is to avoid being upset by the trials and troubles of this life, for these things always tend to contract the heart rather than opening it up to trust God.

Various Thoughts on Prayer

ONE SEARCHES FOR GOD IN books. One finds him in meditation.

All prayers are good when they are accompanied by good intentions and good will.

The Nectar of Life

JUST AS THE BEES SOMETIMES fly great distances without hesitation to reach fields where they have a favorite flowerbed and then, tired but satisfied and laden with pollen, return to the honeycomb to complete the fertile and silent work of transforming the nectar of flowers into nectar of life, so must you, after having gathered it, meditate on it with attention, examine its elements, and search for the hidden meaning. It will then appear to you in all its splendor; it will acquire the power of doing away with your natural materialistic inclinations; it will have the virtue of transforming them into pure and sublime ascensions of the spirit, which will bring together ever more closely your heart with the divine heart of your Lord.

Turn to Prayer in Weakness

The spirit indeed is willing, but the flesh is weak.

—MATTHEW 26:41

I EXHORT YOU TO APPROACH [God] with filial trust and selfless love. He loves you, and you return this love as best you can. He desires nothing else, and you must confide in him, pray, hope, and love him always. Do not be disheartened by…physical and moral suffering.

It is true that sometimes the spirit is ready to do the will of God whereas the flesh is weak, but console yourself because Jesus wants the spirit and not the flesh. In fact, in his fully accepted agony in the Garden, the humanity of Jesus also felt human nature's repugnance for suffering, so that he prayed to the heavenly Father to remove the chalice, if it were possible; and if this repugnance was overcome, it was due to prayer.

Thank you, Lord, for Padre Pio's reminder that I cannot avoid fear and repugnance for what faces me at times, but I can always find a way through it if I keep praying.

Don't Dwell on Past Misdeeds

IN OUR THOUGHTS AND AT confession we must not dwell on sins that have been already confessed. Because of our contrition Jesus has forgiven them at the tribunal of penance. There he faced us and our miseries like a creditor in front of a debtor. With a gesture of infinite generosity he tore up and destroyed the bills we signed with our sins, which we could certainly not have paid without the help of his divine clemency. To go back to these sins, to bring them up again just to have them forgiven again, because of doubt that they were really and abundantly remitted, would this not be considered a lack of trust in the goodness which he proved by his tearing up every document of debt contracted through sin?

Dwell on them, if it is a source of comfort for your soul. By all means think of the offenses against justice, wisdom, and the infinite mercy of God, but only for the purpose of weeping redemptive tears of repentance and love.

Exhaustion

For we do not want you to be ignorant, brethren, of the affliction we experienced in Asia; for we were so utterly, unbearably crushed that we despaired of life itself.

—2 CORINTHIANS 1:8

YOU ASK ME TO REPLY to you at length, and I would like to please you, but, dear God, up to now I have been working indefatigably for twenty hours, and one o'clock in the morning has already struck while I write you this letter. At this stage I am exhausted, and I cannot go on much longer.... Do not let the brevity of my letter cause you to doubt my concern for you. My arms are tired from continually raising them to heaven in order to tear graces from the Lord for you.

Pray at All Times

Pray at all times in the Spirit, with all prayer and supplication. To that end keep alert with all perseverance, making supplication for all the saints.

—EPHESIANS 6:18

PRAYER IS THE BEST WEAPON we have; it is the key to God's heart. You must speak to Jesus not only with your lips but with your heart; in fact, on certain occasions you should speak to him only with your heart.

Lord, I want to pray, but I get distracted. When I am not thinking of you, Lord, let every beat of my heart be an act of love for you, let my hands sing your praises in their work, however menial, and may every breath I take call to your Spirit.

Intercessory Prayer

Continue steadfastly in prayer, being watchful in it with
thanksgiving.

—COLOSSIANS 4:2

OH, HOW I HOPE THAT my poor [prayers] for you will all be
granted by the Lord! I know it is only Jesus who probes the
depths of your soul; only Jesus has a full knowledge of your
desires and needs. Therefore, I constantly present and recommend you to him, and I beg him to satisfy your desires.

*In the mystery of your providence, you call me to intercede in
prayer for certain people. You alone know the depths of their souls
and their true needs. Time and again I lift them, Lord, into your
transforming light and nourishing, redemptive love. And I cry for
them, as for myself, "Heal us, O Lord, and bless us!"*

Praying in the Spirit

The Holy Spirit, whom the Father will send in my name...
will teach you all things.

—JOHN 14:26

PADRE PIO ASKED A DIRECTOR:

How is it, Father, that when I am with Jesus I do not remember
everything I had firmly resolved to ask him? Yet I feel sincerely
sorry for this absentmindedness. How is this to be explained?

* * *

In another letter, Pio, recognizing the power of the Spirit,
prays:

May the grace of the divine Spirit be more and more super-
abundant in your heart.

*It seems common, Lord, in your saints to be so guided by your Holy
Spirit as to who and what they intercede for that they may forget
to ask graces for someone in spite of a firm resolve to do so. Jesus,
may I, too, be docile to the Holy Spirit in my prayers.*

Guardian Angels

PADRE ALESSIO PARENTE REMEMBERED:

Being at Padre Pio's side for almost six years, I often heard it said:

"Father, as I will not be able to come to see you again, what should I do if I need your prayers?" And Padre Pio would reply: "If you cannot come to me, send me your Guardian Angel. He can take a message from you to me and I will assist you as much as I can."

One day, [as] I was sitting by his side, Padre Pio [was] fingering his rosary. There was such a peace and calm around him that I felt encouraged to ask some questions. To my surprise, [he replied]:

"Come on, my son, leave me alone. Don't you see that I am very busy?"

"Strange," I thought.... While I remained totally silent thinking it was not true that he was busy, Padre Pio turned to me and said: "Didn't you see all those Guardian Angels going backwards and forwards from my spiritual children bringing messages from them?"

I retorted: "Father, I have not seen even one Guardian Angel, but I believe you because you tell people every day to send you theirs."

Don't Worry

And now, little children, abide in him.

—1 JOHN 2:28

PRAY, HOPE, AND DON'T WORRY. Worry is useless. God is merciful and will hear your prayer.

Lord, keep me in your peace, free from anxiety and worry, which accomplish nothing and only sap my strength. I do trust in you, Lord, with all my will. Help me when my feelings, against my will, succumb to anxiety.

On Temptation

Lead us not into temptation but deliver us from evil.

—MATTHEW 6:13

YOU MUST TURN TO GOD when [tempted]; you must hope in him and expect everything that is good from him. Don't voluntarily dwell on what the enemy presents to you. Remember that he who flees wins, and at the first sign of aversion for those [particular] people, you must stop thinking of it and turn to God. Bend your knee before him and with the greatest humility say this short prayer: "Have mercy on me, a poor weakling." Then get up and with holy indifference go about your business.

When Prayer Is Hard

We do not know how to pray as we ought.

—ROMANS 8:26

YOU TELL ME THAT ON account of your sleepy, distracted, fickle, and most wretched soul, frequently with the addition of physical complaints, you cannot bear to remain in church for [very long after Mass to pray]. Don't worry on this account. Make an effort to overcome vexation and boredom, and don't weary your mind excessively with very long and continued prayers when your heart and mind are not so inclined.

...When possible...in the silence of your heart and in solitude, offer your praises, your blessings, your contrite and humble heart, and your entire self to the heavenly Father.

Even for a Saint, God May Seem Absent

[He] alone stretched out the heavens,
and trampled the waves of the sea;

…

Lo, he passes by me, and I see him not;
he moves on, but I do not perceive him.

—JOB 9:8, 11

PIO COMPLAINED TO A DIRECTOR:
I am praying continually, but my prayer will never rise up from this lowly world. Dear Father, heaven seems to me to have turned to stone; an iron hand rests on my head and thrusts me further and further away.

Doing One's Best in Prayer

And when you pray, you must not be like the hypocrites; for they love to stand and pray in the synagogues and at the street corners, that they may be seen by men. Truly, I say to you, they have their reward. But when you pray, go into your room and shut the door and pray to your Father who is in secret; and your Father who sees in secret will reward you. And in praying do not heap up empty phrases as the Gentiles do; for they think that they will be heard for their many words. Do not be like them, for your Father knows what you need before you ask him.

—MATTHEW 6:5–8

IT IS TRUE THAT, GIVEN our condition, it is not within our power to keep our thoughts always fixed on God, but let us do our best to keep ourselves, as far as possible, in his presence. This we can and must do, calling to mind every now and then the great truth that God sees us.

The Prayer Groups

IN 1943, AS THE WAR was at its deadliest, Pius XII sent out a heartfelt appeal for people to gather in groups and pray. Padre Pio took the pope's call to heart and thus were born the Padre Pio prayer groups—simple get-togethers for the sole purpose of prayer under the direction of a priest. This undertaking spread all over the world. At the time of Pio's death, there were 726 prayer groups in 20 countries, with a total membership of just under 70,000 members.

True prayer always leads to deeds of charity. Members of these prayer groups became particularly involved in the charitable works promoted by Padre Pio.

Ecstasy

THE OCCASIONS ON WHICH I can use my intellect in discursive prayer and avail of the activity of my senses are becoming increasingly rare…. The soul placed in this state by the Lord and enriched with much heavenly knowledge ought to be more eloquent, but it isn't; it has become almost speechless. I don't know if this is something which happens to me alone. In very general terms and more often than not in words which are empty of meaning, my soul succeeds in expressing some small part of what the Spouse of souls is accomplishing within it…. All this is no slight torment for my soul.

It is like what might happen to a poor little shepherd boy who found himself brought into a royal chamber where there was an infinite number of precious objects such as he had never seen before. He would like to tell others about all he had seen; he would muster all his intellectual and cognitive powers to do so, but finding all efforts useless to make himself understood, he would prefer to keep silence. This is what usually happens to my soul, which by divine goodness alone has been raised to this degree of prayer.

An Incident in Pietrelcina

THE YOUNG PADRE PIO WAS returning, in the late evening, in the company of the parish priest, Don Salvatore Pannullo, from the Pietrelcina cemetery. When they arrived [at the place] where today stands the Capuchin friary with the adjoining seminary and church, dedicated to the Holy Family, Padre Pio, as if immersed in thought and in prophetic tone, said to the priest: "Don Salvatore, what a beautiful fragrance of incense and sound of angels singing! Can you hear it?" Don Salvatore, surprised, responded: "Piuccio [an affectionate name for Pio], are you mad or dreaming? There is no smell of incense or sound of angels singing!" Then Padre Pio said: "Father! One day there will rise on this spot a friary and church from where there will ascend to the Lord the incense of prayer and hymns of praise!"

The parish priest, who knew of Pio's holiness, answered: "Well, if it is the will of God."

History proved Padre Pio right.

Praying That the Kingdom Come

I GIVE HEARTFELT THANKS TO the heavenly Father, through our Lord, Jesus Christ, for the constantly new graces with which he continues to enrich your soul. Oh, may he always be blessed by all his creatures.... May God's reign come soon; may this most holy Father sanctify his Church; may he abundantly shower his mercy on those souls who have not known him up to now.

May he destroy the reign of Satan and reveal, to the confusion of this infernal beast, all his evil snares; may he reveal, to all slaves of this awful wretch, what a liar he is. May this most tender Father enlighten the intelligence and touch the hearts of all men, so that the fervent may not become cooler or slow down in the ways of salvation, that the lukewarm may become more fervent, and those who have moved far from him may return. May he also...confuse all the wise of this world, so that they do not wage war and inhibit the propagation of his reign.

Finally, may this most holy Father banish from the Church all the dissension that exists and impede the birth of more so that there will be only one sheepfold and only one Shepherd. May he multiply a hundredfold the number of chosen souls, send us many saints and learned ministers, and sanctify those we already possess. May he, through them, make fervor return to all Christian souls. May the number of Catholic missionaries increase as we once again have reason to complain to the divine Master: "The harvest is plentiful, but the laborers are few...." Don't ever forget to pray for these needs.

• FIVE •

Longing for God

WITH ALL HIS BEING, PIO longed for God. From early youth God was his passion. Sometimes Pio enjoyed the divine embrace, but there was never total fulfillment. Always he felt the call to greater intimacy, to greater union. In one early period, he longed for death, asking certain people to pray for this.[3]

In his frustration, death seemed the only means to fulfill his painfully unfulfilled longing, even though at times in this same period he experienced God so rapturously he thought he would die from inability to hold the divine sweetness. When God seemed to have left for other parts, Pio's unsatisfied hunger kept him searching, hoping, longing for God.

....

3. Suicide would not have entered his mind, but if his spiritual directors had let him, he might have died by letting go of life psychologically.

His whole life was a pursuit of the Lover, the spouse of the friar's soul. Even if himself unfulfilled, paradoxically, decade after decade, he brought others into relationship with God through letters, the confessional, and sometimes face-to-face spiritual direction. For this, he offered sacrifices, including his unfulfilled life, as reparation and intercession. Having known God, even incompletely, he thirsted to carry everyone to the refreshing, divine "springs of living water" (Revelation 7:16–17).

Searching for God

As a hart longs
  for flowing streams,
so longs my soul
  for you, O God.

—PSALM 42:1

BUT WHAT IS THIS PAINFUL searching for God that occupies your heart incessantly? It is the effect of the love that draws you and the love that impels you.

My soul longs for you because you call me through your Spirit, speaking wordlessly in my heart; you call me through the beauty of the natural world; and you call me through my inner demand for love and meaning. Speak, Lord, I am listening!

Belonging to God

With my whole heart I seek you;
let me not wander from your commandments!

—PSALM 119:10

HE WHO BELONGS ONLY TO God seeks nobody but God himself, and given that he is equally great in times of tribulation and prosperity, one lives calmly in the midst of adversity.

He who belongs only to God continually thinks of him in the midst of all the events of this life and always tries to become better in the eyes of God, and finds and admires God in all creatures, exclaiming with St. Augustine: "All creatures, O Lord, tell me to love you."

Lord, St. Thérèse of Lisieux said, I only have today—this moment even—to love you. So, as the old prayer says, may every beat of my heart today be an act of love for you.

Kissing Jesus: Living What We Profess

I URGE YOU TO UNITE with me and draw near to Jesus with me, to receive his embrace and a kiss that sanctifies and saves us.... The prophet Isaiah said: For to us a child is born, to us a son is given (Isaiah 9:6). This child...is the affectionate brother, the most loving Spouse, of our souls, of whom the sacred spouse of the Song, prefiguring the faithful soul, sought the company and yearned for the divine kisses: O that you were like a brother to me.... If I met you outside, I would kiss you.... O that you would kiss me with the kisses of your mouth! (Song of Solomon 8:1; 1:2).

This son is Jesus, and we can kiss him without betraying him, give him the kiss and the embrace of grace and love he expects from us and which he promises to return. We can do all this, St. Bernard tells us, by serving him with genuine affection, by carrying out in holy works his heavenly doctrine, which we profess by our words.

Let us not cease, then, to kiss this divine Son in this way, for if these are the kisses we give him now, he himself will come to take us in his arms and give us the kiss of peace in the last sacraments at the hour of death. Thus we shall end our life in the holy kiss of the Lord...which, according to St. Bernard, is not a matter of approaching face-to-face and mouth-to-mouth. Rather does it mean that the Creator draws close to his creature, and man and God are united for all eternity.

The Desire to Love God
Is the Love of God

YOU BECOME SAD AT THE love you feel for God. It seems to you that it is little more than nothing.... Well, you should know, my dear daughter, that *in divino* the desire to love is love.

Who placed this yearning to love the Lord in your heart? Don't holy desires come from above? Are we perhaps capable of arousing in ourselves one single desire of that kind without the grace of God which sweetly works within us? If there was nothing but the desire to love God in a soul, everything is present already; God himself is there, because God is not, nor can he be, anywhere except where there is a desire for his love.

Rest assured as regards the existence of divine love in your heart. And if this desire of yours is not satisfied; if it seems to you that you always desire without possessing perfect love, all this signifies that you must never say "enough!"; we cannot and must not stop on the path of divine love.

Pio Guides a Spiritual Child

I URGE YOU TO PRAY continually to the heavenly Father that He may always keep you close to His divine Heart, [so] that He may make you hear His loving voice more and more clearly and lead you to correspond with increasing gratitude. Ask Jesus with boundless confidence, like the bride in the Song of Solomon, to draw you after Him and let you smell the fragrance of his anointing oils [Song of Solomon 1:3–4] so that you may follow swiftly with all the faculties of your soul and body wherever He goes [Revelation 14:4]....

No, your love is not indolent, nor is it sterile. You ought rather to say that you love your heavenly Bridegroom, but that you want that love to grow continually....

Oh, how far you are from that which your feelings would lead you to believe! You love this most tender Spouse, but this seems very little to you because you desire to love with a perfect and consummate love. To us wretched and unfortunate mortals this love, at least in its fullness, is only granted in the next life. O wretched condition of our human nature! May our heavenly Spouse break through this thinnest of thin veils which separates us from Him and grant us at last that perfect love....

The Way to Holiness

Let all bitterness and wrath and anger and clamor and slander be put away from you, with all malice, and be kind to one another, tenderhearted, forgiving one another, as God in Christ forgave you.

—EPHESIANS 4:31–32

BE WATCHFUL, I TELL YOU, and never place too much trust in yourself or count excessively on your own strength. Try to advance more and more on the way to perfection and practice charity more and more, for charity is the bond of Christian perfection.

Do not worry, however, for the good we endeavor to do to others will also result in the sanctification of our own souls.

St. Paul tells us what we must renounce, Lord. But it is impossible to simply say, "I will not feel angry," or, "I will not feel bitterness." Such things must be gifts of grace.

The Transcendence of God

As a young Capuchin, Pio confided in his spiritual director: On…occasions, although I am not thinking of such a thing at all, my soul goes on fire with the most keen desire to possess Jesus entirely. Then with an indescribable vividness communicated to my soul by the Lord, I am shown as in a mirror my whole future life as nothing but a martyrdom. Without knowing why, and with unspeakable love, I yearn for death. Despite all my efforts I am driven to ask God with tears in my eyes to let me be taken from this exile. I feel inflamed with such a lively and ardent desire to please God and am gripped by such a fear of falling into any slightest imperfection that I would like to flee from all dealings with creatures.

Simultaneously, however, another desire rises up like a giant in my heart, the longing to be in the midst of all peoples, to proclaim at the top of my voice who this great God of mercy is. Now and then…the Lord [also] grants me certain pleasures that even I myself do not understand. The happiness I experience is so extreme that I would like to share it with others so that they might help me to thank the Lord.

Again, when I am busy about even indifferent things, a mere word about God or the sudden thought of some such word affects me so deeply that I am carried out of myself. Then the Lord usually grants me the grace of revealing to me some secrets, which remain indelibly impressed on my soul. I am unable, however, to describe [them]...for...I have no adequate words for the purpose. Even the secrets which I succeed to some extent in putting into words lose so much of their splendor that I regard myself with compassion and disgust.

Transformed but Not Perfect

And we all, with unveiled face, beholding the glory of the Lord, are being changed into his likeness from one degree of glory to another; for this comes from the Lord who is the Spirit.

—2 CORINTHIANS 3:18

But we have this treasure in earthen vessels, to show that the transcendent power belongs to God and not to us.

—2 CORINTHIANS 4:7

I BELIEVE YOU SHOULD TAKE a little rest and carefully consider the inconstancy of the human spirit and how easily it becomes embarrassed and agitated. I believe that all the spiritual agitation you suffered in the past was caused by nothing but a great desire to arrive quickly at an imaginary perfection, made with excessive haste.

Let me explain further: Your imagination was intent on reaching a total perfection to which your will wished to lead you. But more often than not it is terrified by the great difficulty and impossibility of reaching this.

The Fire of Love

With my whole heart I cry; answer me, O LORD!
  I will keep your statutes.
I cry to you; save me,
  that I may observe your testimonies.
I rise before dawn and cry for help;
  I hope in your words.
My eyes are awake before the watches of the night,
  that I may meditate upon your promise.
Hear my voice in your steadfast love;
  O LORD, in your justice preserve my life.

—PSALM 119:145–49

IN THE LAST FEW DAYS more than in the past I have felt within me an indescribable uneasiness. The loving anxiety with which my soul rushes toward God has been deeper and more intense for some days now and produces deep down in me an unspeakable ardor. Moreover, since this fire sometimes leaps up to an enormous height in my soul, I yearn so intensely for God, it seems as if all my bones were dried up by this longing.

Ask to Be Holy

Blessed be the God and Father of our Lord Jesus Christ, who has blessed us in Christ with every spiritual blessing in the heavenly places, even as he chose us in him before the foundation of the world, that we should be holy and blameless before him.

—EPHESIANS 1:3–4

AS REGARDS YOUR...BEHAVIOR IN church, do not fear. The most useful, fruitful, and also the most acceptable way to the Lord is precisely that: To ask Jesus to make us holy is neither presumption nor audacity, because it is the same as desiring to love him greatly. The fears that arise, as to whether you spent your time in the presence of God well or otherwise, are without foundation. And dwelling on this is a true waste of time that could be used for holier and more fruitful matters.

The Heart May Love More Than Mind Perceives

He brought me to the banqueting house,
and his banner over me was love.

—SONG OF SOLOMON 2:4–5

WHAT I UNDERSTAND MOST TRULY and clearly is that my heart loves to a much greater extent than my intellect perceives. Of this alone I am certain, and I have never had the slightest doubt about it. Moreover, I do not believe I am telling an untruth when I say that I have never been tempted in this respect. I am so perfectly sure that my will loves this most tender Spouse that, apart from Holy Scripture, I am certain of nothing else to the same degree to which I am certain of this.

What a great thought, Lord: that perhaps my heart loves steadfastly as my will desires in spite of my intellect's doubts and restlessness. Surely to know you, Lord, is to love you. I love you now but not nearly as much as you deserve to be loved. Give me more love, Lord, to love you with!

God's Touch

I KEEP MY EYES FIXED on the East, in the night which surrounds me, to discover that miraculous star which guided our fore-bears to the Grotto of Bethlehem. But I strain my eyes in vain to see that luminary rise in the heavens. The more I fix my gaze the dimmer my sight becomes; the greater my effort, the more ardent my search, the deeper the darkness which enve-lopes me.

Only once did I feel in the deepest recesses of my spirit something so delicate that I do not know how to explain it to you. Without seeing anything, my soul became aware of his presence and then, as I would describe it, he came so close to my soul that I felt his touch. To give you a feeble image of it, it was like what happens when your body feels the pressure of another body against it.

I was seized with the greatest fear, [but] by degrees this fear became a heavenly rapture.... I cannot tell you whether or not at that moment I was still aware of being in this body of mine. Only God knows.

To Grow in Love

I BEG YOU IN OUR most tender Jesus not to yield to this fear of not loving God. I understand very well that nobody can worthily love God, but when a person does all he can himself and trusts in the divine mercy, why should Jesus reject one who is seeking him like this?

Say to Jesus, as St. Augustine invariably said: "'Give what you command and command what you will.' Do you want great love from me, Jesus? I too desire this, just as a deer longs to reach a flowing stream, but as you see I have no more love to give! Give me some more and I'll offer it to you!" Do not doubt that Jesus who is so good will accept your offer.

Weaning the Soul

[A CHILD'S] WEANING CAUSES HIM to suffer [but it is necessary so that, properly nourished,] he will become a fine man.

God deals with our souls in this manner. He wants to win us over to himself by having us experience abundant sweetness and consolations in all our devotions. But who does not see the great danger that surrounds this kind of love of God? It is easy for the poor soul to become attached to the [sweetness and consolations], while paying very little attention to [real] love which alone make it dear and pleasing to God.

Our most sweet Lord hastens to the rescue. When he sees that a person has acquired sufficient virtue to persevere in his holy service without the attractions and sweetness which arrive through the senses, he then [offers] that person greater holiness [by removing] the delightful feelings experienced in meditations, prayers, and other devotions.

The Saint's Longing to Be United to God Forever

PIO WROTE TO A SPIRITUAL director:

Since the Lord is prolonging my life, I know this is his will. Yet despite the efforts I make, I very seldom succeed in making an act of real resignation, for I always have before my mental gaze the clear knowledge that only by death is true life to be found. Hence it is that more often than not, unwittingly, I am led to make acts of impatience and utter words of complaint to the most tender Lord to the point of calling him—do not be scandalized, please, Father—of calling him cruel, a tormentor of the souls who desire to love him. But this is not all. When I feel life weighing on me more than ever, when I experience in the depths of my soul something like a most ardent flame which burns without consuming me, then it is that I just cannot bring myself to pronounce a single act of resignation to the divine will in enduring this life. O God, King of my heart, only Source of all my happiness, how much longer must I wait before I can openly enjoy your ineffable beauty?

One Thing Is Necessary

ONE THING IS NECESSARY: TO be near Jesus. You know well that at the birth of our Lord the shepherds heard the angelic and divine chants of the heavenly spirits. The Scriptures say so. But they do not say that his Virgin Mother and St. Joseph, who were nearer to the Child, heard the voices of the angels or saw those miracles of splendor. On the contrary, they heard the Child weeping and saw by the light of a poor lantern the eyes of the Divine Child all bathed in tears, in sighs and shivering with cold. Now I ask you: would you not have preferred to be in the dark stable filled with the cries of the little Child, than with the shepherds, beside yourself with joy over those sweet melodies from heaven and the beauties of this wonderful splendor?

Pride

For...what have you that you did not receive? If then you received it, why do you boast as if it were not a gift?

—1 CORINTHIANS 4:7, *JB*

TO REFUSE TO SUBMIT ONE'S own judgment to that of others, especially to those who are quite expert in the field in question, is a sign that we possess very little docility and an all too obvious sign of secret pride. You know this yourself and you agree with me. Well, then, take heart and avoid falling into this fault again. Keep your eyes wide open for this wretched vice, knowing how much it displeases Jesus, for it is written that God opposes the proud, but gives grace to the humble.

Turn to the Light

Once you were darkness, but now you are light in the Lord; walk as children of light (for the fruit of light is found in all that is good and right and true).

—EPHESIANS 5:8–9

WE ARE NOT ALL CALLED to the same state [of life] and the Holy Spirit doesn't work in all souls in the same way. He "blows as he wills and where he wills" [John 3:8]. Live completely at peace because there will be light.

Jesus, My Food!

Approach me, you who desire me, and take your fill of my fruits, for memories of me are sweeter than honey.... They who eat me will hunger for more, they who drink me will thirst for more.

—ECCLESIASTICUS 24:19–20, *JB*

[ON RECEIVING COMMUNION:] HOW HAPPY Jesus makes me! How sweet is his spirit! I...can do nothing but weep and repeat: "Jesus, my food!"

The Mystery of Jesus as Food and Drink

MY HEART FEELS DRAWN BY a higher force each morning before I am united with him in the Blessed Sacrament. I have such a hunger and thirst before I receive him that I almost die, and...I am incapable of not uniting myself with him.... Moreover, instead of being appeased after I have received him sacramentally, this hunger and thirst steadily increase. When I already possess this Supreme Good, then indeed the abundance of sweetness is so great that I very nearly say to Jesus: "Enough, I can hardly bear any more."

Thirsting for God

Jesus stood up and proclaimed, "If any one thirst, let him come to me and drink. He who believes in me, as the scripture has said, 'Out of his heart shall flow rivers of living water.'"

—JOHN 7:37–38

HOW IS IT POSSIBLE THAT the fountain of living water that issues from the divine Heart should be far from a soul that rushes to it like a thirsty hart? It is true that this soul may also fail to believe it because it feels continually consumed by an unquenchable and insatiable thirst. But what of that? Does this, perhaps, go to show that the soul does not possess God? Quite the opposite. This happens because the soul has not yet reached the end of its journey and is not yet totally immersed in the eternal fountain of his divine love, which will happen in the kingdom of glory.

Let us therefore love to quench our thirst at this fountain of living water and go forward all the time along the way of divine love. But let us also be convinced…that our souls will never be satisfied here below.

A Desire Never Completely Satisfied on Earth

FOR PITY'S SAKE...DON'T THINK me more than I am. It seems to me that I have no charity at all. In the many years I have spent at Jesus' school all the desires I have for the good God have not yet been satisfied. I feel within me all the time something I cannot define, something akin to a void. I would like my love to be more perfect and no matter how much I strive to do this, I continue to feel ever more intensely this desire to love. I understand only too well that this desire can never be completely satisfied as long as we are wayfarers on this earth and this is where all my sufferings [of unrequited longing] start.

Sin Versus Human Weakness

But one is tempted by one's own desire, being lured and enticed by it; then, when that desire has conceived, it gives birth to sin, and that sin, when it is fully grown, gives birth to death. Do not be deceived, my beloved.

—JAMES 1:14–16

THE DEVIL HAS ONLY ONE door through which to enter into our soul: the will. There are no secret doors. There is no sin, if it has not been committed willfully. When the will does not consent, there is no sin but [only] human weakness.

Trying to Love God

YOU COMPLAIN AND DOUBT YOUR love for Jesus. But tell me, whoever was it that told you [that] you do not love our most sweet Savior?

Ah, I know you would like to love God as much as he deserves. But you know, also, that all this is not possible for us creatures. God commands us to love him not as much and as he deserves, because he knows our limitations and therefore he does not ask us to do what we cannot, but rather, he commands us to love him in accordance with our strength; with all our soul, all our mind, and all our heart.

Well, then, don't you make every effort to do this? And even if you don't succeed, why do you complain? Why do you worry? God understands very well our intention, which is upright and holy before him. God knows very well the reason why many good desires are not realized except after having worked a great deal, and some are never realized at all. But not even in this is there a reason to uselessly afflict yourself, because there is always profit...for the soul. Because if nothing but mortification for the soul were gained from this, it would still be a marvelous thing.

An Extremely Pure Divine Light

YOUR STATE OF SOUL IS one of desolation or holy spiritual suffering. I assure you that the knowledge of your interior unworthiness is an extremely pure divine light, in which your potentiality to commit any crime, without divine grace, is placed before your consideration. That light is the result of the great mercy of God and was granted to the saints, because it shelters the soul from all feelings of vanity or pride and consolidates humility which is the foundation of true virtue and Christian perfection.

St. Teresa also received this knowledge and says that it is so painful and horrible that it would cause death if the Lord did not sustain the heart.

This knowledge of your potential unworthiness must not be confused with that of true unworthiness. You are mistaking the one for the other. You fear you are...that which is only possible in you.

[Remember that] God can reject everything in a creature conceived in sin, but he absolutely cannot reject the sincere desire to love him.

The Weight and the Bliss of Possessing God

I FIND IT ALMOST IMPOSSIBLE to explain the action of the Beloved. He keeps pouring himself completely into the small vase of this creature, and I suffer an unspeakable martyrdom because of my inability to bear the weight of this immense love. How can I carry the Infinite in this little heart of mine? How can I continue to confine him to the narrow cell of my soul? My soul is melting with pain and love, and bitterness and sweetness simultaneously. How can I endure such immense suffering inflicted by the Most High? [Yet] because of the exultation of possessing him in me, I cannot refrain from saying with the most holy Virgin: "My spirit rejoices in God my Savior" [Luke 1:47]. Possessing him within me, I am impelled to say with the spouse of the Sacred Song: "I found him whom my soul loves; I held him and would not let him go" [Song of Solomon 3:4].

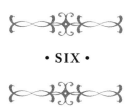

• SIX •

Victory in Spiritual Warfare

Pio was also a warrior. In a vision at fifteen, the terrified teen was impelled by Christ to fight a giant adversary—clearly the devil. After the boy's victory, the Savior said battles with this adversary would be the youth's life, but he promised always to help.

As a young Capuchin, if his adversary could not make Pio sin, he tried to induce despair through physical attacks God permitted in two forms: fearsome bodily assaults and a mysterious TB-like illness that brought Pio near death.

Visible stigmata strangely brought bodily health, but then Pio battled unjust persecutions and spiritual darkness. Toward his life's end, new physical disabilities developed, including asthma. As with everyone, bodily illness affected Pio's soul and mind. Struggling to breathe, he fought anxieties, including the fear of being a burden to the brethren.

His battles raised Pio to ever-higher degrees of sanctity. By his offering each suffering to God for others, many escaped darkness by receiving physical, emotional, and spiritual healing, or by triumphing over unrelieved suffering, like Pio, through grace.

Padre Pio, in my own struggles of body, soul, and mind, pray for me!

"The Indomitable Spirit of a Warrior"

JOURNALIST GIAMBATTISTA ANGIOLETTI WENT TO San
Giovanni expecting to see "a little friar." Instead he said when
Padre Pio approached he appeared as "an ancient warrior
with a dark tunic open at the collar." Angioletti was "dumb-
founded at the unexpected appearance of the man who was
full of energy and vigor and who, instead of speaking of heavenly things [to him], spoke of…present-day-politics; of agri-
cultural reform; raging against the lazy, the cowardly…." The
journalist wrote, "like lightning, I had the certainty that true
faith springs from energy. Furthermore…from violence, from
the indomitable spirit of a warrior. In order to tear evil from
the hearts of men, two things only are adequate; first sweetness, and then strength, and this is irreplaceable…. One of
these without the other can do nothing."

Follow Bravely in the Footsteps of the Saints

To keep me from being too elated by the abundance of revelations, a thorn was given me in the flesh, a messenger of Satan, to harass me, to keep me from being too elated. Three times I besought the Lord about this, that it should leave me; but he said to me, "My grace is sufficient for you, for my power is made perfect in weakness." I will all the more gladly boast of my weaknesses, that the power of Christ may rest upon me.

—2 CORINTHIANS 12:7–9

[DON'T LET] THE COUNTLESS TEMPTATIONS with which you are continually assailed frighten you, because the Holy Spirit forewarns the devout soul who is trying to advance in the ways of the Lord, to prepare itself for temptations. ("My son, if you come forward to serve the Lord, prepare yourself for temptation," Sirach 2:1).

Therefore, take heart because the sure and infallible sign of the health of a soul is temptation. Let the thought that the lives of the saints were not free from this trial, give us the courage to bear it.

[St. Paul] the apostle of the people, after being taken away to Paradise, was subjected to such a trial that Satan went so far as to hit him (see 2 Corinthians 12:7, above). Dear God! Who can read those pages without feeling one's blood freezing? How many tears, how many sighs, how many groans, how many prayers did this holy apostle raise, so that the Lord might withdraw this most painful trial from him!

But what was Jesus' reply? Only this: "My grace is sufficient for you" (2 Corinthians 12:9). One becomes perfect in weakness.

Therefore take heart. Jesus makes you also hear the same voice he allowed St. Paul to hear. Fight valiantly and you will obtain the reward of strong souls.

Gaining Ground

DO NOT HAVE A GREAT desire to be freed from the trial: A soldier must gain a great deal in war before he wants it to end.... True peace does not consist in fighting but in winning. Those who have been beaten no longer fight, but just the same they have no true peace.

Come on, we must humble ourselves greatly, seeing that we are not masters of ourselves to any great extent and greatly love comfort and rest.

On Sexual Impurity

Finally, be strong in the Lord and in the strength of his might. Put on the whole armor of God, that you may be able to stand against the wiles of the devil.

—Ephesians 6:10–11

Even in these holy days the enemy is making every effort to induce me to consent to his impious designs. In particular this evil spirit tries by all sort of images to introduce into my mind impure thoughts and ideas of despair. He shows me a most dismal picture of my life, especially my life in the world.

To put it briefly, dear Father, I am right in the grip of the devil, who is trying with all his might to snatch me from the hands of Jesus. I am alone in this combat, and my heart is filled with terror. What is to become of me, I do not know. I feel very weak in mind and body, Father, but I abandon myself in God's hands.

Seeing God

The angel of the Lord appeared to him [Moses] in a flame of fire out of the midst of a bush…and lo, the bush was burning, yet it was not consumed. And Moses said, "I will turn aside to see this great sight, why the bush is not burnt." When the Lord saw that he turned aside to see, God called to him out of the bush, "Moses, Moses!" And he said, "Here am I." Then he said, "Do not come near; put off your shoes from your feet, for the place on which you are standing is holy ground." And he said, "I am the God of your father, the God of Abraham, the God of Isaac, and the God of Jacob." And Moses hid his face, for he was afraid to look at God.

—Exodus 3:2–6

I am convinced that I must speak to you [God] in the midst of thunder and hurricanes, that I should see you in the burning bush amid the fire of tribulations, but to do all this I see that it is necessary to take off one's shoes and give up entirely one's own will and affections.

The Terrors of God

For the arrows of the Almighty are in me; my spirit drinks their poison; the terrors of God are arrayed against me.

—JOB 6:4

THE SPIRITUAL COMBATS, INSTEAD OF dying down, are pressing on me relentlessly. Darkness is followed by darkness, and spiritual blindness has become pitch darkness for me.... I haven't the strength to speak to you this time about my spiritual state. My present state of soul is such that I couldn't conceive a more deplorable one, and what is worse, I have lost all hope of seeing the sun rise again before I enter into eternal rest. The feeling is very strong within me that I must arrive at the *Consummatum est*. This feeling pervades my whole being, and if I suffer on this account it is solely due to the fear that I will not be able to bear up under this most harsh trial until the end. Do not tell me that the Lord will help me, because I have only myself to blame and am fully aware of the enormity of my wickedness in the Lord's sight.

O the Blessed Angels!

HOW CONSOLING IT IS TO know [that] one is always under the protection of a heavenly spirit who never abandons us, not even (what an admirable thing!) when we are actually offending God! How delightful is this great truth to the one who believes! Who is to be feared, then, by the devout soul who is trying to love Jesus, when accompanied by such an illustrious warrior? Was he not, perhaps, one of the multitude who joined with St. Michael…to defend God's honor against Satan and all the other rebellious angels?… Well, then, let me tell you that he is still powerful against Satan and his satellites. His love has not lessened, and he can never fail to defend us.

Make a habit of thinking of him…. When it seems to you that you are alone and abandoned, don't complain that you are without a friend to whom you can open your heart and confide your woes. For goodness' sake, don't forget this invisible companion who is always there to listen to you, always ready to console you.

Call to God in Trouble

WAR HAS BEEN DECLARED UPON you...you need to be watchful at every moment, to put up a strong defense, with the eye of faith always fixed on the God of hosts, who is fighting along with you and for you. You must have boundless faith in the divine goodness, for the victory is absolutely certain.

How could you think otherwise? Isn't our God more concerned about our salvation than we are ourselves? Isn't he stronger than hell itself? Who can ever resist and overcome the King of the heavens? What are the world, the devil, the flesh, and all our enemies before the Lord?

Sacrificial Service to Souls

YOU MUST KNOW THAT I do not have a free moment: A crowd of souls thirsting for Jesus fall upon me, so that I don't know which way to turn. Before such an abundant harvest, on one hand I rejoice in the Lord, because I see the ranks of elect souls always increasing and Jesus loved more; and on the other hand I feel broken by such a weight.

There have been periods when I heard confessions without interruption for eighteen hours consecutively.

The Surest Test of Love

HE WHO BEGINS TO LOVE must be willing to suffer.

Don't be daunted by the cross. The surest test of love consists in suffering for the loved one. If God suffered so much for love, the pain we suffer for him becomes as lovable as love itself. In the troubles which the Lord bestows on you, be patient and conform yourself gladly to the divine Heart in the knowledge that all is a continual game on the part of your Lover.

The more you are afflicted the more you ought to rejoice, because in the fire of tribulation the soul will become pure gold, worthy to shine in the heavenly palace.

[Human nature] naturally wants to escape [suffering], for man was created to enjoy happiness. As long as we remain in this world we shall always feel a natural aversion for suffering. Be quite sure that if in the apex of our spirit, we submit to it for love of God, [our humanity's natural aversion] becomes a cause of merit for us if we hold it in check and subdue it.

The Crown Is Won in Combat

Our commonwealth is in heaven, and from it we await a Savior, the Lord Jesus Christ, who will change our lowly body to be like his glorious body, by the power which enables him even to subject all things to himself.

Therefore, my brethren, whom I love and long for, my joy and crown, stand firm thus in the Lord, my beloved.

—PHILIPPIANS 3:20–21; 4:1

THE STORM THAT IS RAGING around you is a sure sign of love. This is not just a personal conviction of mine, but an argument from Scripture which tells us that temptations are proof of the soul's union with God: "My son, when you are about to serve God, prepare yourself for temptations" (Sirach 2:1). It is an indication of God's presence deep down in the soul. "I will be with him in trouble," says the Lord (Psalm 91:15:3). Therefore the apostle St. James exhorts souls to rejoice when they see themselves tormented by various calamities and numerous contradictions: "Count it all joy, my brethren, when you meet various trials" (James 1:2–4).

The reason is that the crown is won in combat. If we realize that every victory we obtain has a corresponding degree of eternal glory, how can we fail to rejoice, my dearest daughter, when we find ourselves obliged to face many trials in the course of our life?

May this thought console you, my daughter, and may you be encouraged by the example of Jesus who in every respect has been tempted as we are, yet without sinning (Hebrews 4:15).

* * *

Don't be disheartened if...nature cries out for comfort. Jesus' human nature also asked that the chalice might be taken away.

From Hundreds of Letters

IN A 1917 LETTER TO a family named Ventrella, with whom he was friends, Pio encouraged three sisters:

Tell me once again, my dear daughters, what are you afraid of? Oh don't you hear God saying to Abraham and to you: "Do not fear; I am your protector" [Genesis 15:1]. What do you seek on earth, O daughters, if not God? You already possess him. Therefore be firm in your resolutions; stay in the ship in which he has placed you, and let the storm and hurricane come. Long live Jesus! You will not perish. He may sleep, but in the right place and at the right time he will awaken to restore the calm. Therefore, my daughters, do not fear, you are walking on the sea amidst the wind and waves, but with Jesus.

What is there to fear then? But, if fear takes you by surprise, exclaim strongly with St. Peter, "Oh Lord, save me!" He will stretch out his hand to you; hold it tightly and walk joyfully. Let the world turn upside down; let everything be in darkness, smoke, and noise, God is with us.

Heaven

LET US ALWAYS KEEP BEFORE our eyes the fact that here on earth we are on a battlefield and that in paradise we shall receive the crown of victory; that this is a testing-ground, and the prize will be awarded up above; that we are now in a land of exile, while our true homeland is heaven, to which we must continually aspire. Let us live, then...with a lively faith, a firm hope, and an ardent love, with eyes fixed on heaven and the keenest desire, as long as we are travelers, to dwell one day in heaven whenever this is pleasing to God.

On the Angels

Because you have made the LORD your refuge,
  the Most High your habitation,
no evil shall befall you,
  no scourge come near your tent.
For he will give his angels charge of you
  to guard you in all your ways.

—PSALM 91:9–11

I CANNOT TELL YOU THE way these scoundrels [devils] beat me. Sometimes I feel I am about to die. On Saturday it seemed to me that they intended to put an end to me.... I turned to my angel, and after he had kept me waiting a while, there he was hovering close to me, singing hymns to the Divine Majesty....

I rebuked him bitterly for having kept me waiting so long when I had not failed to call him to my assistance. To punish him, I did not want to look him in the face.... But he, poor creature, caught up with me almost in tears and held me until I raised my eyes to his face and found him all upset.

Then, "I am always close to you, my beloved young man," he said. "I am always hovering around you with the affection aroused by your gratitude to the Beloved of your heart. This affection of mine will never end, not even when you die. I know that your generous heart beats all the time for the One we both love; you would cross every mountain and every desert in search of him, to see him again, to embrace him again in these extreme moments, and to ask him to break at once this chain that unites you to the body.... For the present [he cannot give you your desire], but do not cease to ask him insistently for this, because his supreme delight is to have you with him...."

Poor little angel! He is too good.

Test the Spirits

THE OTHER NIGHT THE DEVIL appeared to me in the likeness of one of our fathers and gave me a very strict order from Father Provincial not to write to you [my spiritual director] anymore, as it is against poverty and a serious obstacle to perfection.... I wept bitterly, believing this to be a fact. I should never have even faintly suspected this to be one of the ogre's snares if the angel had not revealed the fraud to me.

God Faithfully Cares for Me

HAS THE LORD NOT TOLD us that he is faithful and promised never to allow us to be vanquished? God is faithful.... How could you persuade yourself of anything else, my dear sister? Isn't our good God far above anything we can conceive? Isn't he more interested than we are in our salvation? How many times has he not given us proof of this? How many victories have you not gained over your very powerful enemies and over yourself, through the divine assistance, without which you would inevitably have been crushed? Let us consider Jesus' love for us and his concern for our well-being, and then let us be at peace.

Glory Beyond All Comparison

JESUS IS ALWAYS WITH YOU, even when you don't feel his presence. He is never so close to you as he is during your spiritual battles. He is always there.

For pity's sake, I beseech you not to wrong him by entertaining the slightest suspicion that he has abandoned you even for a single moment. This is really one of the most diabolical temptations which you must drive far from you as soon as you are aware of it.

Let it be a consolation to know, my dear, that the joys of eternity will be all the more heartfelt and profound, the more numerous the days of humiliation and the years of unhappiness we have known in the present life. This is not just my own opinion. Holy Scripture offers us infallible testimony. [The Psalmist says] "Make us glad as many days as Thou hast afflicted us, and as many years as we have seen evil" (Psalm 90:15). St. Paul the apostle, moreover, [says,] "This slight momentary affliction is preparing us for an eternal weight of glory beyond all comparison" (2 Corinthians 4:17).

Weaving My Designs

Be patient, therefore, brethren, until the coming of the Lord. Behold, the farmer waits for the precious fruit of the earth, being patient over it until it receives the early and the late rain. You also be patient.

—JAMES 5:7–8

PROVERBS PRAISES THE STRONG WOMAN: "She puts her hands to the distaff, and her hands hold the spindle" [Proverbs 31:19]. I willingly tell you something on this point. Your distaff is the multitude of your desires. Little by little every day you weave your designs until it is finished and you will come out on top. But beware of haste because you would knot the yarn and entangle the spindle.

Wings That Lift Us to God

HUMILITY AND PURITY OF CONDUCT are the wings which raise us up to God and in a manner deify us. Remember this: the sinner who is ashamed to do evil is closer to God than the upright man who is ashamed to do good.

Ignore Ridicule

For consider your call, brethren; not many of you were wise according to worldly standards, not many were powerful, not many were of noble birth; but God chose what is foolish in the world to shame the wise, God chose what is weak in the world to shame the strong, God chose what is low and despised in the world, even things that are not, to bring to nothing things that are, so that no human being might boast in the presence of God. He is the source of your life in Christ Jesus, whom God made our wisdom, our righteousness and sanctification and redemption; therefore, as it is written, "Let him who boasts, boast of the Lord."

—1 Corinthians 1:26–31

Be always faithful to God in keeping the promises made to Him, and do not bother about the ridicule of the foolish. Know that the saints were always sneered at by the world and worldlings; they have trampled them under foot and have triumphed over the world and its maxims.

Of Suffering and Relief

But rejoice in so far as you share Christ's sufferings, that you
may also rejoice and be glad when his glory is revealed.

—1 PETER 4:13

I HAVE A GREAT DESIRE to suffer for the love of Jesus. How is
it, then, that when I am put to the test, altogether against my
will I seek relief? What force and violence must I use toward
myself in these trials to reduce nature to silence when it cries
out loudly, so to speak, for consolation!

We're in a War

Be sober, be watchful. Your adversary the devil prowls around like a roaring lion, seeking some one to devour. Resist him, firm in your faith.

—1 Peter 5:8–9

Do you know what the devil has resorted to? He didn't want me to inform you in my last letter about the war he is waging on me. And since, as usual, I did not want to listen to him…they…(there were several of them although only one spoke)…hurled themselves upon me, cursing me and beating me severely.

Let's Thwart Satan—by Forgiving

Any one whom you forgive, I also forgive. What I have forgiven, if I have forgiven anything, has been for your sake in the presence of Christ, to keep Satan from gaining the advantage over us; for we are not ignorant of his designs.

—2 CORINTHIANS 2:10–11

YOU WILL NEVER COMPLAIN ABOUT offences, no matter where they come from, remembering that Jesus was saturated with ignominy from the malice of men he himself aided. You will excuse everyone with Christian charity, keeping before your eyes the example of the divine Master, who excused even his crucifiers before the Father.

Human Weakness and God's Grace

I FELT THE TWO FORCES within me, who were struggling amongst themselves and lacerating my heart: the world that wanted me for itself, and God who was calling me to a new life. Dear God! Who could explain that interior martyrdom that was taking place within me? The very thought of that interior struggle...makes the blood freeze in my veins, and twenty years have passed now....

I heard the voice of duty to obey you, oh true and good God; but your enemies and mine oppressed me, dislocated my bones, scoffed at me, and tortured my heart! Oh my God, my Spouse, I wanted to obey you.

You know, O Lord, of the warm tears I shed before you during those extremely doleful times! You know, oh God of my soul, of the groanings of my heart.... But you, Lord, who made this son of yours experience all the effects of true abandonment, arose in the end; you held out your powerful hand to me and led me there, to where you had first called me. O my God, may infinite praise and thanks be rendered to you.

Try to Take the Eternal View

I am the Lord your God, who brought you out of the land of Egypt, out of the house of bondage. You shall have no other gods before me.

—EXODUS 20:2–3

THE CHILDREN OF ISRAEL WERE in the desert for forty years before they reached the Promised Land, even though six weeks were more than sufficient for this journey. Nonetheless it was not right to question why God led them along winding and bitter paths, and all those who did so died before they arrived there. Even Moses, a great friend of God, died on the border of the Promised Land, which he saw from a distance without being able to enjoy it [Deuteronomy 34].

Don't pay too much attention to the path on which you are walking. Keep your eyes always fixed on he who guides you and on the heavenly homeland to which he is leading you. Does it matter whether you get there by way of the desert or through fields, as long as God is with you, and that you finally possess blessed eternity?

SEVEN

Faith

GOD'S GREATEST GIFT TO PADRE Pio was faith and the trust in God that comes from faith. God could work miracles through Pio *because* he was a man of faith.

Faith, Pio would be the first to stress, is not an attribute or achievement, but a gift from God, one that is "caught more than taught." That grace for Pio began by being born into "the family for whom God is everything," as someone characterized Papa and Mama Forgione. Pio's parents modeled faith even when it was costly. Beyond these human influences, Pio was schooled in faith from early childhood by supernatural visions and dialogues, which were proved genuine by their fruits. Like Jesus' agonizing in the garden, faith did not spare Pio from feeling abandoned by God at times and having to cling to faith by acts of the will.

Rather than look down on those of us with less faith, Pio gave his all that we others might find and grow faith, too. He emphasized, "if you want more faith, ask God for it."

Spending time with Pio also lets people "catch" more faith. May this happen to us!

Don't Worry about Tomorrow

I RECOMMEND TO YOU TO HAVE a firm and general proposal to always serve God with all your heart; do not worry about tomorrow. Think about doing good today. And when tomorrow comes, it will be today and then you can think about it. Trust in Providence. It is necessary to make provisions of Manna for only one day and no more. Remember the people of Israel in the desert.

Trusting God

Trust in the LORD with all your heart,
  and do not rely on your own insight.
In all your ways acknowledge him,
  and he will make straight your paths.

—PROVERBS 3:5–6

HOW HAPPY ARE THOSE SOULS who live by faith; who adore the holy plan of God in everything.

Place all your cares in him alone, because he has very great care of you.

Lord, today I will make frequent acts of trust in you.

Lord, Save Me!

O DAUGHTER OF LITTLE FAITH, I also repeat to you with the divine Master, Why are you afraid? No, do not fear; you are walking on the sea amid the wind and waves, but be sure that you are with Jesus. What is there to fear? But if fear takes you by surprise, you too shout loudly: "O Lord, save me!" He will stretch out his hand to you; and this hand is precisely that tenuous ray of trust in him which you feel in the depths of your soul. Squeeze his hand tightly and walk joyfully, at least in the apex of your soul.

Without divine grace, could you have been victorious in all the crises and all the spiritual battles which you have had to face? Well, then, open your soul more and more to divine hope, have more trust in the divine mercy which is the only refuge of the soul exposed to a stormy sea.

The Holy Spirit: Bringer of Good to Those Who Seek God

NEVER FALL BACK ON YOURSELF alone, but place all your trust in God, and don't be too eager to be set free from your present state. Let the Holy Spirit act within you. Give yourself up to all his transports and have no fear. He is so wise and gentle and discreet that he never brings about anything but good. How good this Holy Spirit, this Comforter, is to all, but how supremely good he is to those who seek him!

Invitation to the Full Life

And in that region there were shepherds out in the field, keeping watch over their flock by night. And an angel of the Lord appeared to them, and the glory of the Lord shone around them, and they were filled with fear. And the angel said to them, "Be not afraid; for behold, I bring you good news of a great joy which will come to all the people....

—LUKE 2:8–10

Now when Jesus was born in Bethlehem of Judea in the days of Herod the king, behold, wise men from the East came to Jerusalem, saying, "Where is he who has been born king of the Jews? For we have seen his star in the East, and have come to worship him."

—MATTHEW 2:1–2

JESUS CALLS THE POOR AND simple shepherds by means of angels to manifest himself to them. He calls the learned men by means of their science. And all of them, moved interiorly by grace, hasten to adore him. He calls all of us with divine inspirations, and he communicates himself to us with his grace.

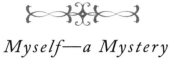

Myself—a Mystery

For now we see in a mirror dimly, but then face to face. Now I know in part; then I shall understand fully, even as I have been fully understood.

—1 Corinthians 13:12

To put it briefly: My belief is a great effort of my poor will, against all human reasoning on my part. Perhaps it is for this reason that I will never be able to receive any solace…. This, my dear Father [and spiritual director], is not a matter of several times a day but is continual, and if I were to act differently I could not help becoming unfaithful to my God. The night is growing ever darker, and I don't know what the Lord has in store for me.

There are so many things that I would like to tell you, Father, but I am unable to do so. I realize that I am a mystery to myself.

Lord, let me remain a mystery to myself so long as you become clearer and clearer in my spiritual vision, to lead me away from sin and ego into the person you want me to be.

How Hard It Is to Believe!

AN INFINITE NUMBER OF FEARS assail me at every moment.
Temptations against faith which would drive me to deny
everything. My dear Father, how hard it is to believe!

There are times, moreover, when I am assailed by violent
temptations against faith. I am certain that my will does not
yield, but my imagination is so inflamed and presents the
temptation in such bright colors that sin seems not merely
something indifferent but even delightful.

Away with Discouragement

I BESEECH YOU WHOLEHEARTEDLY NOT to waste time in thinking about the past. If it was used well, let us give glory to God; if badly, let us detest it and confide it to the goodness of the heavenly Father. In fact, I exhort you to tranquilize your heart with the consoling thought that [the] part of your life not well spent has already been forgiven by our most sweet God.

Flee with all your strength the perturbations and anxieties of the heart, otherwise all your efforts will bear little or no fruit at all. We may be sure that if our spirit is agitated, the devil's assaults will be more frequent and direct, because…he plays on our natural weaknesses. We must be careful on this important point. As soon as we are aware of becoming discouraged, we must revive our faith and abandon ourselves in the arms of the divine Father, who is always ready to receive us—always, that is, if we go to him sincerely.

The Affability of Jesus

THERE ARE MOMENTS WHEN I call to mind the severity of Jesus and am about to feel distressed, but then when I consider his affability, I am completely consoled. I cannot help abandoning myself to this tenderness, this happiness.

I trust Jesus so completely that even if I were to see hell open before me and find myself on the brink of the abyss, I should not lose confidence. I should not despair but continue to trust in him.

Of Birds and Souls

You open your hand,
   you satisfy the desire of every living thing.

—PSALM 145:16

Even the sparrow finds a home,
   and the swallow a nest for herself,
   where she may lay her young,
at your altars, O LORD of hosts,
   my King and my God.

—PSALM 84:3

LISTEN TO WHAT I AM thinking: I consider what writers say about the kingfisher, little birds who build their nests on the beach near the sea. They build it in a circular form and so tightly compressed that the seawater cannot penetrate it. Above it is an opening from which they receive air. Here these graceful little birds place their young ones, so that when the sea comes upon them by surprise, they can swim with confidence and float on the waves without being filled with water or submerging. And the air they breathe through that opening serves as a counterbalance so that those little balls of fluff are not overturned.

My daughter, may Jesus deign to make you understand the meaning of this example of mine. I want your heart to be like this: well compact and closed on all sides, so that if the worries and storms of the world, the evil spirit, and the flesh come up on it, it will not be penetrated. Leave but one opening to your heart that is toward heaven....

How I love and am enraptured by those little birds.... They swim like fish and sing like birds. But what amazes me most of all is that the anchor is cast above them and not below, in order to strengthen them against the waves.

May this poor writing of mine raise your exceedingly down-cast spirit and make it ascend to him who is the source of all consolation.

Lord, this man-made world of freeways and appointments screens your natural world. I forget to look at the squirrel on my fence, the bulbs breaking through the still cold soil. I forget to bless the trees and bow down before the beauty of your sunsets. Let me see past the man-made world, Lord, to your world in all its intricate and incredible beauty. And give me again a child's eye, "looking up filled with wonder like a cup." For when I truly see your world, I see you.

Reject Sadness, Cultivate Joy

WHEN YOU ARE OVERCOME BY sadness…then more than ever must you renew your trust in God…. Cast far from you all thought of things that cause you to be sad, refuse to harbor all such thoughts just as you would reject temptations against holy purity. You must not dwell any longer on these tormenting thoughts.

…In addition you must endeavor to occupy your mind with happy things. Try to dwell, for example, on the goodness of the heavenly Father in giving you his Only Begotten Son, on the beauty of our holy faith, on the happiness reserved for us in paradise, on the resurrection and ascension of Jesus, on the glory he enjoys in paradise and which, if we remain faithful to him, he has reserved one day for us also. Try to have other people keep you company, moreover, and avoid topics that tend to make you sad. Let your speech be edifying, and confine yourself to cheerful topics.

Keep Running

For I am already on the point of being sacrificed; the time of my departure has come. I have fought the good fight, I have finished the race, I have kept the faith.

—2 TIMOTHY 4:6–7

ON THE OTHER HAND, THIS knowledge [of God's loving plans for you] must serve as an incentive to lay aside all fear and not come to a halt halfway on your journey, because of the sufferings and trials that must be endured if you are to reach the end of this extremely long road…. Run, then, without growing weary, and may the Lord direct and guide your steps so that you may not fall. Make haste, I tell you, for the road is long and time is very short.

Lord, even for those who live a long time, life is short. And our day of departure can come anytime. Help me to endure and keep the faith until the end, whenever it comes. Jesus, I place my life in your hands!

The Dark Night of the Soul

My God, my God, why have you forsaken me?
  Why are you so far from helping me, from the words of my
  groaning?
O my God, I cry by day, but you do not answer;
  and by night, but find no rest.

—PSALM 22:1–2

FAREWELL TO THE DELIGHTS WITH which the Lord had inebriated my soul! Where is that enjoyment of the adorable divine presence? Everything has disappeared from intellect and spirit. It is a continual desert of darkness, dejection, apathy; this is the native land of death, the night of abandonment, the cavern of desolation. Here the soul is far from its God and left to itself.

My soul continues to groan beneath the weight of this night.… It is incapable of thinking of supernatural things.… My will seems to make an effort to love, but in a flash, dear Father, it becomes hard and motionless as a stone. My memory tries to take hold of something to console it, but all in vain.…

What increases my torment more than anything is the occasional vague remembrance of having previously known and loved this same Lord whom I now feel I neither know nor love.... I then try to find at least in creatures the traces of the One for whom my soul longs, but I no longer recognize the usual image of him who has abandoned me. It is precisely at this point that my soul is overcome by terror, and no longer knowing what to do to find its God, it wails bitterly to the Lord: My God, my God, why have you abandoned me?

Help for the Troubled Heart

Let not your hearts be troubled; believe in God, believe also in me.

—JOHN 14:1

LIVE CALMLY, AND DO NOT worry excessively, because in order to work more freely in us, the Holy Spirit needs tranquility and calm. And for you, every anxious thought is a mistake, as you have no reason to fear. It is the Lord who works within you, and you must do nothing except leave the door of your heart wide open so that he might work as he pleases.

Lord, help me to feel to the bottom of my being that "every anxious thought is a mistake," as St. Pio counseled one of his spiritual children. I cannot always control my feelings, Lord, but I tell you with my will that I love you, trust you, and surrender all that I am and have to you.

God's Light

This is the message we have heard from him and proclaim to you, that God is light and in him is no darkness at all.

—1 JOHN 1:5

THE FINEST GRACE THAT CAN be asked by and on behalf of those who aspire to the spiritual life [is]…an increase of heavenly light. This is a light that cannot be acquired either by prolonged study or through human teaching, but which is directly infused by God. When the righteous soul obtains this light, it comes to know and love its God and eternal things in its meditations with extreme clarity and relish. Although it is nothing but a light of faith, it is still sufficient to produce such spiritual consolation that the earth, in the first place, disappears from view, while all that this world can offer is seen to be worthless.

Dear Lord, grant me this light so I may love you, as Pio says, "with extreme clarity and relish."

God Alone

Preserve me, O God, for in you I take refuge.
  I say to the Lord, "You are my Lord;
  I have no good apart from you."

—PSALM 16:1–2, 5

DON'T BE DISCOURAGED IF YOU experience spiritual dryness. This does not mean that the Lord has abandoned you.... All that is happening in your soul is due to the exquisiteness of Jesus' love for you. He wants you entirely for himself, he wants you to place all your trust and all your affection in him alone, and it is precisely for this reason that he sends you this spiritual aridity, to unite you more closely to him, to rid you of certain little attachments which do not appear as such to us and which, in many cases, we do not even recognize or detect.

The House of the Lord

ENTER THE CHURCH IN SILENCE and with great respect, considering yourself unworthy to appear before the Lord's Majesty.... Remember that our soul is the temple of God, and as such we must keep it pure and spotless before God and his angels. Let us blush for having given access to the devil and his snares many times (with his enticements to the world, his pomp, his calling to the flesh) by not being able to keep our hearts pure and our bodies chaste; for having allowed our enemies to insinuate themselves into our hearts, thus desecrating the temple of God, which we became through holy baptism. Then take holy water and make the sign of the cross carefully and slowly.

As soon as you are before God in the Blessed Sacrament, devoutly genuflect. Once you have found your place, kneel down and render the tribute of your presence and devotion to Jesus in the Blessed Sacrament. Confide all your needs to him, along with those of others. Speak to him in filial abandonment, give free rein to your heart, and give him complete freedom to work in you as he thinks best.

Gaining Ground

What does it profit, my brethren, if a man says he has faith but has not works? Can his faith save him? If a brother or sister is ill-clad and in lack of daily food, and one of you says to them, "Go in peace, be warmed and filled," without giving them the things needed for the body, what does it profit? So faith by itself, if it has no works, is dead.

—JAMES 2:14–17

YES, LET US DO GOOD. Now is the time for sowing, and if we want to reap an abundant harvest, it is not so necessary to sow a lot of seed as to scatter it in good ground. We have already sown a lot of seed, but it counts for very little if we want to be gladdened at harvest time. Let us sow now and continue to sow, my dear, and let nothing grieve us on this account. Let us make sure that this seed falls in good soil, and when the heat arrives to burst it open and bring forth a plant, we must still be on the watch and take good care that the weeds do not smother the young plants.

Faith in the Lord

THANKS TO THE FAVORS WITH which God fills me incessantly, I have greatly improved as regards my trust in him. In the past it sometimes seemed to me that I needed the help of others, but this is no longer the case. I know from my own experience that the best way to avoid falling is to lean on the cross of Jesus, with confidence in him alone, who for our salvation desired to be nailed to it.

Lord, even your great friends, saints like Padre Pio, must grow in trust and faith. How encouraging! Lord, help me to trust you more and more, until my trust in you equals that of your saints.

Hope in God

I...EXHORT YOU AGAIN TO be trustful. A soul who trusts in her Lord and places all her hope in him has nothing to fear. The enemy of our salvation is always around us to snatch from our hearts the anchor that is to lead us to salvation, by which I mean trust in God our Father. Let us keep a very firm hold on this anchor and not relinquish it for a single moment. Otherwise all would be lost. Repeat continually, and more especially in the darkest hours, those most beautiful words of Job: Even if you are to slay me, O Lord, I will still hope in you. Always be on your guard and don't become puffed up, considering yourself to be good in any way or above others. Don't imagine that you are better than them or at least as good, but consider all to be better than yourself. The enemy...overcomes the presumptuous and not the humble of heart.

Padre Pio and a Young Pole

WHEN WORLD WAR II ENDED, in 1945, a young Pole, who had done his priestly studies in secret right under the eyes of Poland's Nazi occupiers, came to Rome for post-ordination studies. Father Karol Wojtyla made a pilgrimage to San Giovanni Rotondo and went to confession to Padre Pio.

According to Padre Joseph Pius Martin of Our Lady of Grace Friary, Wojtyla had countered the claim that Padre Pio told him at that time that he would be pope one day. But whatever their exchange, Wojtyla left San Giovanni Rotondo confirmed in devotion to Padre Pio as a great man of God.

Fifteen years later, the Polish priest was a bishop spending a lot of time in Rome for the Second Vatican Council. True to his vow of total poverty, at this time Padre Pio had given The Home for the Relief of Suffering to the Vatican. Weekly, a layman employed by the Vatican came to San Giovanni to meet with Padre Pio regarding the hospital. In Rome, Bishop Wojtyla asked this layman, Angelo Battisti, if he would take a note to Padre Pio. The note the Polish prelate handed Battisti asked Padre Pio's prayers for a friend of the Bishop's—a laywoman. The mother of four girls and a concentration camp survivor, she was dying of terminal cancer.

When Battisti gave Padre Pio the card, the Capuchin read it and remarked, "We cannot refuse him."

A few days later, Bishop Wojtyla sent a second note with Angelo Battisti to Padre Pio. Written by hand on a little white card, the note thanks Padre Pio on behalf of himself, the cancer patient, her husband, and her daughters for her complete cure.

Padre Pio told someone, "File away those cards." So, surmised Padre Joseph Pius, Padre Pio must have known what lay in the future for Poland's brilliant young bishop.

As Pope John Paul II, Wojtyla remained devoted to Padre Pio. He visited San Giovanni Rotondo again as a cardinal and, later, as pope. And it was he who beatified and canonized Pio, with thanks to God for that privilege.

As for the two little white cards that mark a miracle, they are housed today in the archives at San Giovanni Rotondo.

Remain at Peace

TO A FRIEND DYING OF cancer:

I beg you, for heaven's sake, to calm your anxiety and apprehension.... Remain at peace, continue to go forward, and don't let your swift course be stopped when I assure you in our most tender Lord that you are already halfway to the summit of Calvary. It is true that this is the darkest hour of the night for you, but may the thought of a bright dawn and a more brilliant noontime sustain you, cheer you up, and induce you to keep on moving forward. Do not doubt that the One who has sustained you so far will continue with ever greater patience and divine kindness to support you on the remainder of your difficult and trying journey.

The Journey

When they had heard the king they went their way; and lo, the star which they had seen in the East went before them, till it came to rest over the place where the child was.

—MATTHEW 2:9

FAITH ALSO GUIDES US, AND we follow securely in its light the way which leads to God, his homeland, just as the holy Magi, guided by the star, symbol of faith, reached the desired place.

· EIGHT ·

On Relationships

LIKE EVERY SAINT, PADRE PIO'S foremost relationship was and is with God.

Burning with desire for the One who is love, beauty, truth, and all perfection, Pio searched for God, found his joy in God, and willingly humbled himself—accepting the mortification of visible stigmata—to serve God. At God's call, he battled to rescue souls from darkness, obeying his superiors as to *how* he might fight at any given time.

A good dad to his God-given spiritual children, he taught them life's meaning, ranked its values, and provided practical tips for success in arriving at heaven's door—where his fatherly hope was to wait until he was able to enter with the last one. Meantime, he mirrored God's call to them and to us: with God's help, seek God, love God, and offer love and appropriate service to everyone.

On fire with God's love, Pio was certainly open to *all* God's children—whether a wife-beating atheist God sent him to convert, a friend whose egotism he lovingly corrected, or a recently-deceased woman whose holiness he venerated. Of her he wrote, "Holiness shone forth from her and made her the…most lovable image of God."

Some use those words of Pio himself.

True Love

If anyone says, "I love God," and hates his brother, he is a liar; for he who does not love his brother whom he has seen, cannot love God whom he has not seen. And this commandment we have from him, that he who loves God should love his brother also.

—1 JOHN 4:20–21

HOLINESS MEANS LOVING OUR NEIGHBOR as ourselves for love of God. In this connection holiness means loving those who curse us, who hate and persecute us, and even doing good to them. Holiness means living humbly, being disinterested, prudent, just, patient, kind, chaste, meek, diligent; carrying out one's duties for no other reason than that of pleasing God; and receiving from him alone the reward we deserve.

I see, Lord, that you are a God of relationships. You invite me to the deepest intimacy with you; and in that intimacy I, one with you, am to offer Jesus to the world, "that they might have life and have it to the full."

Imitating Our Saints

Precious in the sight of the Lord
  is the death of his saints.

—PSALM 116:15

I HEARD OF OUR VERY dear Francesca's departure for the heavenly homeland before you told me about it. I shed a lot of tears at the loss of such a precious, not to say rare, existence. These tears were and are being shed solely because of the not inconsiderable loss the Church militant [that is, the Christians still on earth] has suffered by her death. An immense sense of veneration surges over me at the thought of this departed one, and almost without my being aware of it, I feel induced to kneel down as if before a sacred image. Holiness shone forth from her and made her the most perfect and most lovable image of God.

You whose enviable lot it was to draw near to this truly holy soul will agree with what I have said about her. How many times when you were close to her, when you heard her speak and considered the way she acted and all that she was, have you not forgotten all about yourself, felt small and wretched, and experienced a strange sense of admiration, veneration, and joy that cannot be put into words? How often, I say, when you were beside her, have you not felt closer to God and an indefinable need to become better?

She has now disappeared from our bodily sight, but let us make her live on within us by imitating her in the practice of virtue and holiness.

Lord, I thank you with all my heart for the now dead holy friends and relatives you have given me over my lifetime. They demonstrated the virtues by the way they lived and made me want to conquer my failings and become a better person. May they bask now in the glory of your presence. And may you make me holy, too, Lord—however impossible that seems at times—so that I may come where they are and be reunited with them in you.

The Marvel of a Faithful Friend

A faithful friend is a sturdy shelter:
  he that has found one has found a treasure.
There is nothing so precious as a faithful friend,
  and no scales can measure his excellence.
A faithful friend is an elixir of life;
  and those who fear the Lord will find him.

—SIRACH 6:14–16

MAY JESUS ALWAYS BE THE peaceful King of your heart, and may he grant you all the spiritual benefits you desire and earnestly wish for the souls of others. Amen.

At the approach of your beautiful name day I feel welling up in my heart more than ever a sense of most lively gratitude to you, the one who has been concerned more than anyone else about my spiritual progress. I give praise to God for all this, and to you I return my infinite thanks, while I solemnly promise to repay you, as far as this is in my power, by grateful prayer to God for all the good you have done me.

For your feast day please accept my most sincere and earnest good wishes, which come from the bottom of my heart, especially for your progress in the spiritual life. May God be pleased to grant my earnest wishes, which are always that you may be preserved in holy love. May he grant me the happiness of seeing you advance more and more in the ways of the Lord.

Lord, I am struck by how grateful Pio was to his friend, particularly for that friend's concern for Pio's spiritual progress, and how his own desires for good things for his friend were also completely spiritual. I have been blessed with many friends, Lord, and I thank you for every one of them. Help my friendship never to lead anyone away from you, Lord. May those I love who do not know you find in me an invitation to make your acquaintance. And for those who have led me closer to you or mirrored something of your beauty and love, I thank you, Lord, with all my heart.

Make Our Heavenly Father Proud

LIVE IN SUCH A WAY that the heavenly Father may be proud of you, as he is proud of so many other chosen souls. Live in such a way that you may be able to repeat at every moment with the apostle St. Paul: "Be imitators of me, as I am of Jesus Christ" (1 Corinthians 4:16; 11:1). Live in such a way, I repeat, that the world will be forced to say of you: "Here is Christ." Oh, for pity's sake, do not consider this an exaggeration! Every Christian who is a true imitator and follower of the fair Nazarene can and must call himself a second Christ and show forth most clearly in his life the entire image of Christ. Oh, if only all Christians were to live up to their vocation, this very land of exile would be changed into a paradise!

A Heart of Gold

PADRE PELLEGRINO OF S. ELIA a Pianisi, who had the joy of living at Padre Pio's side, speaks of Pio's "heart of gold."

Padre Pio's heart!... I am unable to describe the gentle harmony that God's Spirit breathed within him. To me, he was an eternal child, rejoicing in the surprises that were brought to him, from the taking of tobacco to being offered a chocolate. He enjoyed the delicate pleasures of friendship, purified and assured by poverty. He was most sensitive to the slightest courtesy, which he repaid with prayers and graces for eternal life. He was most acute of mind and with the sensitivity of a mimosa. He perceived from a distance the desires of men, and replied to those who loved him, with immediacy. Even the Friary dog was aware of this: if he found the door... open, he would take a walk as far as Padre Pio's room, scratch a moment near the door and would only go away when Padre Pio said: "Beh, that's enough now, you can go."

The Villagers' Defense

[THE LOCAL] BISHOP SENT A formal petition to Rome against Pio. It was full of untruths, including that the friars were using Pio to collect money from the ignorant and credulous. That June, the Holy Office ordered Pio be moved from Our Lady of Grace to some remote friary where the crowds could not find him.

Pio held obedience in such high esteem that he could say, "For me the voice of my Superiors is the voice of God" [which had never kept him from arguing with Benedetto like any son with his father over the latter's directives]. Informed now, he replied he was ready to leave at once.

But the removal, ordered and tried repeatedly over the next few years, proved not so simple. Cynics could claim it was because Pio had put San Giovanni Rotondo on the map and had already begun providing livelihoods for the locals who were renting out their beds and serving meals to the visitors. The more pious, like Pio's spiritual daughters, insisted it was because they weren't about to lose the blessing of having a saint in their midst to shrive their sins, marry, christen, bury, and otherwise lead them to God.

In either case—and probably both were involved—whenever someone arrived who the people of San Giovanni Rotondo thought might have come to transfer Pio, local menfolk took up arms and surrounded the friary. One wild young man actually pointed a gun at Pio and said, "Try to take him and he's a dead man."

For Pio to leave Our Lady of Grace simply proved impossible.

Padre Bill

WHEN HE WAS A YOUNG man, Bill Martin was planning a visit to Europe. His Catholic travel agent said, "Don't you want to visit the priest with the stigmata?" Bill shrugged. He was a "Sunday Mass" kind of Catholic. ("And usually late for that," Bill adds.) To him, a priest with the stigmata was like the Eiffel Tower—just another of Europe's "attractions."

Arriving in San Giovanni Rotondo, however, the New Yorker experienced such a powerful attraction to the mountain village—solely because of the elderly Padre Pio—that he reshuffled his itinerary to stay longer.

Five years later Bill returned, joining the community as a Third Order Franciscan. Thus he shared the last three years of the saint's life, sometimes assisting him with his physical needs as Pio became more feeble.

Of living with Padre Pio, Padre Joseph Pius [formerly Bill Martin] says, "After the timidity wore off, you lived a very simple daily life with this great saint because, in his profound humility, he had no airs or assumption of graces. He never made you feel inferior to him nor ever asked for anything special. He was a lovely person to live with."

Paying Our Debts in Prayer

I remember you constantly in my prayers.... I long night and day to see you, that I may be filled with joy.

—2 TIMOTHY 1:3–4

HOW CAN I REPAY—I don't say you—but your family, for what you and they have done for me? I do my best to repay this debt in some way with my assiduous prayers before the Lord, and for this reason I offered the Mass I sang last Saturday to the heavenly Father for you and your family.

...How happy I would be if I could personally thank you and your family.

God Inspires Bountiful Sowing

The point is this: he who sows sparingly will also reap sparingly, and he who sows bountifully will also reap bountifully.

—2 CORINTHIANS 9:6

FOR ONE WHO IS INFLAMED with divine love, helping the neighbor in his needs is a fever that consumes him by degrees. He would give his life a thousand times if he could induce a soul to offer one more act of praise to the Lord. I too feel that this fever is eating me up.

Live Together in Peace

Mend your ways, heed my appeal, agree with one another, live in peace, and the God of love and peace will be with you.

—2 CORINTHIANS 13:11

BE LIKE LITTLE SPIRITUAL BEES, bringing nothing into their hives but honey and wax. May your homes be full of sweetness, peace, agreement, humility, and piety as regards conversation.

Lord, I desire so much to love you, to love others, and to love your world and all its creatures. When I find my ego getting in the way, love urges me to continue my walk with you. Send your Spirit to help me conquer in me what I cannot overcome by myself. When my feeble love proves inadequate, give me your love to pass on.

Reconciliation

So if you are offering your gift at the altar, and there remember that your brother has something against you, leave your gift there before the altar and go; first be reconciled to your brother, and then come and offer your gift.

—MATTHEW 5:23–24

I OFFER WARMEST THANKS TO the goodness of the heavenly Father for the reconciliation with your brother and his wife. I ask you now to put aside your pessimistic judgment on this situation. May the Lord continue to use mercy toward you all and grant you the grace of holy perseverance. Get rid of the diabolical thought that you have been the cause of the disagreement that has existed up to the present with your brother. Have we understood one another?

Lord, help me always to be open to reconciliation with anyone, no matter the situation.

Attachment to One's Own Opinions

I appeal to you, brethren, by the name of our Lord Jesus Christ, that all of you agree and that there be no dissensions among you, but that you be united in the same mind and the same judgment.

—1 Corinthians 1:10

Complete my joy by being of the same mind, having the same love, being in full accord and of one mind.

—Philippians 2:2

I'll be certain of your constant progress in the path of holiness to which God, by his goodness alone, has called you…[if] you…take care never to quarrel with anyone, never to contend with anyone whomsoever. If you act otherwise, it means good-bye to peace and charity. To be inordinately attached to your own opinion is invariably a source and beginning of discord. St. Paul exhorts us to be united in the same mind.

Angels to Guard You

"He will give his angels charge of you," and "On their hands
they will bear you up, lest you strike your foot against a stone."
—MATTHEW 4:6

MAY YOUR GOOD GUARDIAN ANGEL always watch over you;
may he be your guide on the bitter paths of life. May he always
keep you in the grace of Jesus and sustain you with his hands,
so that you may not stumble on a stone. May he protect you
under his wings from all the snares of the world, the devil, and
the flesh.

Have great devotion…to this good angel; how consoling it
is to know that near us is a spirit who, from the cradle to the
tomb, does not leave us even for an instant, not even when we
dare to sin. And this heavenly spirit guides and protects us like
a friend, a brother.

…It is extremely consoling to know that this angel prays
without ceasing for us and offers to God all our good actions,
our thoughts, our desires, if they are pure. For pity's sake, don't
forget this invisible companion, always present, always ready
to listen to us, and even more ready to console us. O delightful
intimacy, O blessed company! If we could only understand it!

Always keep him present to your mind's eye. Often remember the presence of this angel; thank him, pray to him, always keep him good company. Open up yourself to him, and confide your suffering to him. Have a constant fear of offending the purity of his gaze. Know this and keep it well imprinted on your mind. He is so delicate, so sensitive. Turn to him in times of supreme anxiety, and you will experience his beneficial help.

God Does Not Abandon His Children

I RECEIVED YOUR LETTER, AND even though I understand the complaints you make, I must not let a point that struck me strongly pass without comment. You say that everybody has abandoned you, including myself. Apart from the abandonment of others, I say that you are wrong in complaining about my having abandoned you. Unfortunately, you anticipated my reprimand for you. We have changed places. Do you remember? You have become so indifferent toward your old [spiritual] director, that you even neglect certain rules, I don't say of Christian obedience, but of common politeness. As regards everything else, God knows if I have ever failed to care for your spiritual good. God knows how much I groaned and sighed, feared and prayed continually for you to Jesus.

The supposed abandonment on the part of God is a pure invention on the part of Satan. Jesus is and will always be yours. Don't abstain from working for the good of others, but neither should you neglect your own spiritual betterment. Jesus will always sustain you in everything.

Good Comes from All *for God's Friends*

We know that in everything God works for good with those who love him.

—ROMANS 8:28

YOU WOULD LIKE ME TO be close to you always during this [trial]…and I don't know what I wouldn't do to keep you here at my side. But if you cannot do so, believe that I am always close to you in spirit. And as I am far away from you in the body, the only advice I can give you is to…simply let the Holy Spirit accomplish what he wants in you. Abandon yourself to his transports, and do not fear. He is so discreet, wise, and sweet that he cannot but do good.

The Know-It-All

[PADRE PELLEGRINO, WHO LIVED WITH Padre Pio for years, recalls:] The sun had already set behind the dark mountain. In the friary orchard, Padre Pio, sitting on a little wall, was surrounded by new and old friends. These were spread out, some sitting, some standing, in the farmyard, [where they threshed]...the grain gathered by the mendicant friars. The subject under discussion that evening was the obligation to study ethics, Christian morality, and, in particular, Catholic morality.

[When the bell rang for prayers] one person who, in my opinion, gave himself too many airs, and who, at times, interpreted even Padre Pio's advice for his own personal use, hurried to have the last word: "Only he who has studied morality in depth will save his soul." Padre Pio, who, after having made a move to rise, sat down again in order to listen to the friend's remark, as if he desired to take it in, finally rose to his feet, stretched out his arm toward the...[speaker], and with a radiant smile said to him: "Don't play the know-it-all."

Let Your Sun Shine on the Good and the Bad

Be sons of your Father who is in heaven; for he makes his sun rise on the evil and on the good, and sends rain on the just and on the unjust.

—MATTHEW 5:45

BE CAREFUL, ABOVE ALL, OF charity toward God, your neighbor, and yourself. Refrain from judging anyone whomsoever, except when it is your duty to do so. In this way you will hold everyone in esteem, and you will also show yourself to be a worthy son of the heavenly Father, who makes his sun shine on the evil and on the good.

Real Holiness

Thanks be to God through Jesus Christ our Lord! So then, I of myself serve the law of God with my mind, but with my flesh I serve the law of sin.

—ROMANS 7:25

PIO COUNSELED A WOMAN FRIEND:
[M]any unfortunate people...experience the sharp conflict within themselves to which a hot temper or lustful desires give rise. They do not want to feel or to harbor those impulses, that ill-feeling toward others, those vivid pictures presented by their imagination, those sensual promptings. Poor things! Quite involuntarily these feelings surge up and produce a conflict within them, so that in the act of wanting to do something right they feel violently impelled towards something wrong.

Some think they are offending God when they feel this violent interior inclination to evil. Take heart, you chosen souls, for in this there is no sin, since the holy apostle himself, a chosen instrument, experienced this dreadful conflict within [see Romans 7:16]. Even when carnal impulses are violently felt, there can be no sin when the will does not consent to them.

In a Time of Loss

A WORD OF COMFORT FOR your extremely great suffering on the departure of your father. May Jesus be pleased to instill a little comfort in your hearts through these poor words of mine. But...shouldn't we adore in all circumstances the Supreme Providence of the heavenly Father, whose advice is holy, good, and lovable? He was pleased to recall from this miserable exile your excellent and very dear father, in order to unite him to himself. Let us confess, my good daughters and sisters, that God is good and that his mercy is eternal. His every will is just, and his decrees are full of lofty mysteries; his pleasure is always holy, and his plans, lovable.

I confess...that I fully understand what the departure of your dear father means. He was a model and example of Christian virtue in our times, when the tendency is to desert the ways of the Lord. This is the confession of my weakness, after having done the will of God. But nevertheless, this resentment was truly vivid, but also perfectly tranquil, because I said along with the prophet David: "I remain silent, O Lord, and don't open my mouth because it is you who have done this" (Psalm 39:9)....

But you would like to know how things went for your dear father before Jesus. What doubt can there be on the eternal kiss that this most sweet Jesus accorded him? Wasn't he a fervent Christian, a practicing Catholic, a model father? Come on.... Away with doubts and fears, which are the fruits of your imaginations, because they have no reason to exist. The virtues that adorned the soul of your dear departed one were too obvious.

The Holy Family

Be very careful about the sort of lives you lead, like intelligent and not like senseless people. This may be a wicked age, but your lives should redeem it.

—EPHESIANS 5:15–16, *JB*

MAY THE HOLY FAMILY NEVER withdraw its loving gaze from you and your family. Model yourselves on it, and you will have peace and spiritual and temporal well-being.

Thank you, Lord, for all the graces of each day, from food to eat and sleep at night, to my family and friends. Thank you for being with us in hard times and joyous ones. May each of us always trust in your mercy and love.

God's Holy Love

In this is love, not that we loved God but that he loved us.

—1 JOHN 4:10

MAY GOD BE THE CENTER of your heart and set it all on fire with his holy love! I never cease to bless the divine mercy for the most holy love he shows toward your soul.

My love for you, Lord, is so paltry next to your love for me. I thank you with all my heart and ask that you set me, too, on fire with your holy love, so I may love others as you love.

A Sweet Reminder

PADRE PIO SAID:

> I belong entirely to everyone. Everyone can say "Padre Pio is mine." I deeply love [all humanity]. I love my spiritual children as much as my own soul and even more. I have regenerated them to Jesus through suffering and love. I can forget myself but not my spiritual children. Indeed I can assure you that when the Lord calls me, I will say to him: "Lord, I will stand at the gates of Heaven until I see all my spiritual children have entered."

In 1968 when Padre Pio died, besides leaving a huge hospital called the Home for the Relief of Suffering, his legacy included 726 prayer groups with 68,000 members. Work in Pio's name continues to this day. To find out more (in the United States) contact the National Centre for Padre Pio in Barto, Pennsylvania:

Our Lady of Grace Chapel & Padre Pio Spirituality Centre
Museum and Cultural Centre
111 Barto Road

P.O. Box 206 (mailing address)
Barto, PA 19504 USA
info@padrepio.org
phone: 610-845-3000
http://www.padrepio.org

Visit www.teleradiopadrepio.it for the latest news of what is happening at the Friary in San Giovanni Rotondo.

Sources

The Fires of Love *Meet Padre Pio,* pp. 24–25.

All about Love *Meet Padre Pio,* p. 127.

Advice on Loving God *Letters II,* pp. 99–100.

Living in God's Love *Letters III,* pp. 827, 824.

Prescription: Boundless Confidence in God's Mercy *Letters I,* p. 461.

The Spirit of God Is a Spirit of Peace *Per la storia. Padre Pio da Pietrelcina,* by Alberto Del Fante, Bologna, 1950, quoted in *Have a Good Day,* ed. Fr. Alessio Parente, third ed. (San Giovanni Rotondo, Italy: Padre Pio da Pietrecina Editions), p. 156.

Let God Bury Our Sins *Consigli-Esortazioni di Padre Pio da Pietrelcina,* p. 18.

Mercy Grants Glory *Letters II,* 261. Among the first people to whom Padre Pio gave extensive spiritual guidance by mail was Raffaelina Cerase, one of the two aristocratic sisters whom Padre Agostino first introduced to Pio by letter. Raffaelina Cerase lived with her older sister in the southern Italian city of Foggia.

Love and the Sick *The Voice of Padre Pio* 27, no. 12, 1997, p. 7.

The Surest Sign of Love *Letters I,* p. 672.

Keep Your Eyes on the Lord *Letters III,* p. 425.

How to Love God More *Letters III,* p. 726.

Loving the Dear God *Letters I,* p. 509.

Love of the Beloved *Letters I,* pp. 1249–1250.

To Love God, Our True Good *Letters II,* pp. 213–214.

The Fire of Love March 26, 1914, letter to Padre Benedetto, Padre Pio's second spiritual director at this time, *Letters I,* pp. 517–518.

God's Love and Human Ingratitude Undated September 1911 letter to Padre Benedetto, *Letters I,* p. 267.

Holy and Unholy Fears *Per la storia: Padre Pio da Pietrelcina,* quoted in *Have a Good Day* (San Giovanni Rotondo, Italy: Our Lady of Grace Monastery, 1975), pp. 27–28.

Love Is from God *Letters III*, pp. 669–670.

To Remain in Christ *Letters I*, p. 330.

The Flame of Divine Love *Letters II*, p. 77.

The Mercy of God *Letters III*, pp. 756–757, *Letters II*, p. 168.

Mercy Amid Misery *Letters I*, pp. 523–524.

Padre Pio's Tact *The Voice of Padre Pio,* p. 27, Summer Number, 1997, p. 7.

Love, Love, Love *Consigli-Esortazioni di Padre Pio da Pietrelcina*, p. 11.

A Man Who Laughed *Meet Padre Pio,* pp. 101–102.

A Heritage of Joy Comment on Giuseppa is by Padre Pio's American spiritual daughter, Mary Pyle, who knew his parents well. It can be found in a reminiscence written by Mary in the friary archives. The comments on Grazio are from materials collected by Padre Alessandro of Ripabottoni and Padre Lino Barbati of Prata, reported by C. Bernard Ruffin in *Padre Pio: The True Story* (Huntington, Ind.: Our Sunday Visitor, 1982), chapter two.

True Joys *Meet Padre Pio,* p. 10.

"Exemplary Novice" Pranks *Meet Padre Pio,* pp. 14–16.

Tears of Happiness April 18, 1912, letter to Padre Agostino *Letters I,* p. 308.

Count It All Joy *Letters II*, p. 68.

The Boy Becomes a Man *Meet Padre Pio,* p. 7.

Cheerful under Trial *Meet Padre Pio,* pp. 52–53.

The Laughter of Happy Men *A Padre Pio Profile*, pp. 112–114, *Meet Padre Pio,* pp. 100–101.

The Satisfactions of Spiritual Parenthood *Through the Year With Padre Pio,* p. 63, *Letters III*, p. 682, *Letters III*, 96, *Meet Padre Pio,* p. 40.

"A Human Being Like Everybody Else" Testimony of Andre Mandato of New Jersey, *A Padre Pio Profile*, p. 51.

Peace *The Voice of Padre Pio* 28, no. 6, (1998), p. 13.

Joy to All of Good Will *Letters III*, p. 470.

Be Joyful! *Through the Year With Padre Pio*, pp. 21–22.

Let's Laugh *Letters III*, p. 118, *Through the Year With Padre Pio*, p. 73.

Specks and Logs *Padre Pio visto dall'interno*, p. 62, *Through the Year With Padre Pio*, p. 132.

A Beautiful Heart Trumps Fine Dress *The Voice of Padre Pio* 27, no. 12, 1997, pp. 16–17.

Laughing at Myself Kathleen Stauffer, "They Knew Padre Pio," *Catholic Digest*, December 1991.

Testimonies *Meet Padre Pio*, pp. 143–144.

A Little Flower A memory by Padre Gerardo of Deliceto, who lived with Padre Pio for years, as told in "Padre Pio's Ordinary Side," by Patricia Treece, *The Tidings*, February 6, 1998, p. 19.

About His Gruffness *A Padre Pio Profile*, p. 57, *Quiet Moments with Padre Pio*, n. 79.

Testing the Mystic's Authenticity The parish priest's letter is reproduced in Padre Alessio Parente's *"Send Me Your Guardian Angel,"* *Padre Pio*, p. 32.

Inexplicable Signs *Letters I*, pp. 264–265.

"My Crucifixion" October 22, 1918, letter to Padre Benedetto, following the visible stigmatization he would bear for fifty years, *Letters I*, pp. 1217–1218, *Meet Padre Pio*, pp. 66–67.

Keeping It Quiet *Meet Padre Pio*, pp. 73–74.

God's Healing through His Saints *The Voice of Padre Pio* 32, no. 1, 2002, 19; the letters from Cardinal Wojtyla, who became Pope John Paul II, are in the friary archives.

The Odor of Sanctity *Meet Padre Pio*, pp. 83–84.

Pio Predicts Future Events by Divine Inspiration *Meet Padre Pio*, pp. 107–109.

A Far-Traveling Man *Meet Padre Pio*, pp. 103, 105–106.

Two Places at Once A Bilocation Testimony from Padre Alberto. Padre Alberto's testimony can be found in the friary archives.

The Vast Spiritual World *Letters II*, p. 221.

Bilocation: Sent as God's Messenger *The Voice of Padre Pio* 30, no. 2, 2000, p. 9.

The Wife Beater *The Friar of San Giovanni: Tales of Padre Pio* by John McCaffrey (New York: Image, 1983), quoted in *Padre Pio: Our Good Samaritan* (San Giovanni Rotondo: Padre Pio da Pietrelcino Editions, 1990), pp. 115–116.

Miracle on a Bus *The Voice of Padre Pio* 28, no. 2, 1998, pp. 11–12.

A Miracle for the Miracle Worker *Meet Padre Pio*, pp. 119–120.

The Resurrection Life Begins *Meet Padre Pio*, pp. 133–134.

A Healing Mystery: Relics Testimony from a letter to the friary quoted in *Meet Padre Pio*, p. 145.

The Case of Agnes Stump Details of Agnes's cure, one of many authenticated healings that have taken place since Padre Pio's death, are in the archives of Our Lady of Grace Friary, San Giovanni Rotondo. A detailed account in English may be found in *Padre Pio: Our Good Samaritan*, pp. 25–30.

God's Healing Power through His Saints Testimony of Rita M. DeNitti from friary archives, quoted in Patricia Treece, *Apparitions of Modern Saints* (Ann Arbor, Mich.: Servant, 2001), pp. 148–149.

Prayer A remark of the Padre's in passing, according to the Padre's spiritual son Father Joseph Pius Martin of Our Lady of Grace Friary, San Giovanni Rotondo, who lived with and assisted him in his later years.

Cry Aloud to God February 28, 1915, letter to Raffaelina Cerase, *Letters II*, p. 377.

The Holy Spirit Guides His Prayer May 19, 1914, letter to Raffaelina Cerase, *Letters II*, pp. 101–102.

Daily Prayer *Letters III*, p. 257.

Padre Pio on the Rosary *Meet Padre Pio*, pp. 35–36.

Prayer, Always Prayer *Meet Padre Pio*, p. 110.

Wait Tranquilly for Heaven's Dew Padre Pio Archives, Capuchin Friary, San Giovanni Rotondo, quoted in *Have a Good Day*, pp. 154–155.

Calm in the Storm *Letters I*, p. 470.

Various Thoughts on Prayer *Consigli–Esortazioni de Padre Pio da Pietrelcina*, p. 40, *Per la storia: Padre Pio da Pietrelcina*, 552, all quoted in *Have a Good Day*, pp. 32, 36.

The Nectar of Life *Tra I misteri della scienza e le luci della fede*, p. 172.

Turn to Prayer in Weakness *Letters III*, pp. 81–82.

Don't Dwell on Past Misdeeds *Tra I misteri della scienza e le luci della fede*, by Giorgio Festa, 1933, quoted in *Have a Good Day*, pp. 69–70.

Exhaustion *Letters I*, pp. 777–778.

Pray at All Times *Consigli-Esortazioni di Padre Pio da Pietrelcina*, p. 40.

Intercessory Prayer *Letters III*, p. 371.

Praying in the Spirit *Letters I*, pp. 638, 730.

Guardian Angels Padre Alessio Parente, *"Send Me Your Guardian Angel,"* pp. 86–97.

Don't Worry *Consigli-Esortazioni di Padre Pio da Pietrelcina*, p. 39.

On Temptation March 2, 1917, letter to Assunta Di Tomaso, *Letters III*, p. 418.

When Prayer Is Hard *Letters II*, p. 189.

Even for a Saint, God May Seem Absent *Letters I*, p. 144.

Doing One's Best in Prayer *Letters III*, p. 257.

The Prayer Groups *Meet Padre Pio*, p. 112.

Ecstasy *Letters I*, p. 518.

An Incident in Pietrelcina "Two Prophecies of Padre Pio," by Padre Gerardo, *The Voice of Padre Pio*, 28, no. 3, 1998, p. 10.

Praying That the Kingdom Come *Letters III*, pp. 63–64.

Searching for God *Letters III*, p. 634.

Belonging to God *Letters III*, p. 527.

Kissing Jesus: Living What We Profess *Letters II*, pp. 506–507.

The Desire to Love God Is the Love of God December 14, 1916, letter to schoolteacher Erminia Gargani, *Letters III*, pp. 669–670.

Pio Guides a Spiritual Child Letter to Raffaelina Cerase, May 19, 1914, *Meet Padre Pio*, pp. 48–50.

The Way to Holiness *Letters II*, p. 274, *Letters II*, p. 400.

The Transcendence of God *Letters I*, pp. 413–414.

Transformed but Not Perfect *Letters III*, p. 684.

The Fire of Love *Letters I*, p. 983.

Ask to Be Holy *Letters III*, p. 253.

The Heart May Love More Than Mind Perceives *Letters I*, p. 469.

God's Touch March 3, 1916, letter to Padre Benedetto.

To Grow in Love April 20, 1915, letter to Raffaelina Cerase, *Letters II*, p. 425.

Weaning the Soul January 9, 1915, letter to Raffaelina Cerase, *Letters II*, pp. 308–309.

The Saint's Longing to Be United to God Forever September 25, 1915, letter to Padre Agostino, *Letters I*, p. 731.

One Thing Is Necessary *Padre Pio: Counsels*, p. 20.

Pride *Letters II*, p. 260.

Turn to the Light *Letters III*, p. 108.

Jesus, My Food! *Letters I*, p. 299.

The Mystery of Jesus as Food and Drink *Letters I*, p. 246.

Thirsting for God *Letters II*, pp. 541–542.

A Desire Never Completely Satisfied on Earth March 30, 1915, letter to Raffaelina Cerase, *Letters II*, p. 401.

Sin Versus Human Weakness Padre Pio Archives, Capuchin Friary, San Giovanni Rotondo.

Trying to Love God *Letters III*, p. 927.

An Extremely Pure Divine Light March 26, 1918, letter to teacher Maria Anna Campanile, one of ten children from a family close to Padre Pio, *Letters III*, pp. 956–958.

SOURCES

The Weight and the Bliss of Possessing God January 12, 1919, letter to
  Padre Benedetto, *Letters I*, pp. 1238–1239.
"The Indomitable Spirit of a Warrior" *Padre Pio of Pietrelcina:
  Everybody's Cyrenean* by Alessandro da Ripabottoni, San Giovanni
  Rotondo, 1987, quoted in *Padre Pio: Our Good Samaritan*, pp.
  111–112.
Follow Bravely in the Footsteps of the Saints September 4, 1916, letter
  to Maria Gargani, *Letters III*, pp. 249–250.
Gaining Ground *Letters III*, p. 750.
On Sexual Impurity *Letters I*, pp. 248–249.
Seeing God *Letters I*, p. 933.
The Terrors of God *Letters I*, pp. 861–862.
O the Blessed Angels! *Letters II*, pp. 420–421.
Call to God in Trouble *Letters II*, p. 87.
Sacrificial Service to Souls From two letters of the post-stigmata
  ministry of the early 1920s quoted in *The Voice of Padre Pio*, 27, no.
  12, 1997, p. 9.
The Surest Test of Love *Consigli-Esortazioni di Padre Pio da Pietrelcina*,
  25, *Letters II*, p. 140, *Letters II*, p. 461.
The Crown Is Won in Combat May 19, 1918, letter to Maria Anna
  Campanile, *Letters III*, pp. 963–964, *Letters II*, pp. 437–438.
From Hundreds of Letters *Meet Padre Pio*, p. 64.
Heaven *Letters II*, p. 470.
On the Angels *Letters I*, pp. 351–352.
Test the Spirits *Letters I*, p. 362.
God Faithfully Cares for Me *Letters II*, p. 152.
Glory Beyond All Comparison August 15, 1914, letter to Raffaelina
  Cerase, *Letters II*, p. 168.
Weaving My Designs *Letters III*, p. 291.
Wings That Lift Us to God *Letters III*, pp. 957–958.
Ignore Ridicule *Padre Pio: Counsels*, p. 28.
Of Suffering and Relief *Letters I*, p. 640.

We're in a War *Letters I*, pp. 345–346.

Let's Thwart Satan—by Forgiving Archives, Our Lady of Grace Friary, San Giovanni Rotondo quoted in *Have a Good Day*, p. 135.

Human Weakness and God's Grace *Letters III*, pp. 1016–1017.

Try to Take the Eternal View *Letters III*, pp. 836–837.

Don't Worry about Tomorrow July 4, 1917, letter to Capuchin seminarians, *Letters IV*, pp. 437–438.

Trusting God *Letters III*, p. 815, *Letters III*, p. 131.

Lord, Save Me! *Letters III*, p. 178, *Letters II*, p. 436.

The Holy Spirit: Bringer of Good to Those Who Seek God *Letters II*, p. 70.

Invitation to the Full Life *Letters IV*, pp. 977–978.

Myself—a Mystery *Letters I*, p. 855.

How Hard It Is to Believe! July 16, 1917, and March 8, 1916, letters to Padre Benedetto.

Away with Discouragement February 9, 1916, letter to a fellow priest called to serve in World War I.

The Affability of Jesus *Letters I*, quoted in *The Voice of Padre Pio*, 28, no. 6, 1998, p. 9.

Of Birds and Souls *Letters III*, pp. 111–112.

Reject Sadness, Cultivate Joy *Letters II*, p. 402.

Keep Running *Letters II*, pp. 316–317.

The Dark Night of the Soul *Letters I*, p. 804.

Help for the Troubled Heart *Letters III*, p. 258.

God's Light *Letters II*, p. 211.

God Alone *Letters II*, p. 141.

The House of the Lord *Letters III*, p. 89.

Gaining Ground *Letters II*, pp. 274–275.

Faith in the Lord *Letters I*, p. 519.

Hope in God *Letters II*, pp. 410–411.

Padre Pio and a Young Pole *Meet Padre Pio*, pp. 115–116.

Remain at Peace *Letters II*, pp. 479–480.

SOURCES

The Journey *Letters IV*, p. 980.

On Faith *Consigli-Esortazioni di Padre Pio da Pietrelcina*, p. 57, quoted in *Have a Good Day*, p. 105. See also *Letters III*, pp. 665–666.

True Love *Letters II*, p. 563.

Imitating Our Saints *Letters III*, pp. 146–147.

The Marvel of a Faithful Friend *Letters I*, p. 705.

Make Our Heavenly Father Proud *Letters II*, p. 168.

The Villagers' Defense *Meet Padre Pio*, pp. 79–80.

Padre Bill *Meet Padre Pio*, pp. 124–126.

Paying Our Debts in Prayer *Letters III*, pp. 866–867.

God Inspires Bountiful Sowing *Letters I*, p. 464.

Live Together in Peace *Letters III*, p. 567.

Reconciliation *Letters II*, p. 480.

Attachment to One's Own Opinions *Letters II*, p. 234.

Angels to Guard You *Letters III*, pp. 84–85.

God Does Not Abandon His Children *Letters III*, p. 379.

Good Comes from *All* for God's Friends *Letters III*, p. 1032.

The Know-It-All *The Voice of Padre Pio*, 28, no. 6, 1988, p. 11.

Let Your Sun Shine on the Good and the Bad *Letters I*, p. 1263.

Real Holiness November 16, 1914, letter to Raffaelina Cerase.

In a Time of Loss *Letters III*, pp. 483–484.

The Holy Family *Letters IV*, p. 1000.

God's Holy Love *Letters I*, p. 1009.

A Sweet Reminder Padre Pio Archives, Capuchin Friary, San Giovanni Rotondo.

Bibliography

Consigli-Esortazioni di Padre Pio da Pietrelcina. Foggia, 1965.

da Baggio, Giovanni. *Padre Pio visto dall'interno. (Le mie visite a P. Pio da Pietrelcina).* Florence: Chiesa, 1970.

da Pobladura, Melchiorre and Alessandro da Ripabottoni, eds. *Letters Volume I: Correspondence With His Spiritual Directors (1910-1922),* third edition. Revised and corrected by Father Gerardo Di Flumeri (San Giovanni Rotondo: "Padre Pio da Pietrelcina" Editions, 1987).

———. *Letters Volume II: Correspondence With the Noblewoman Raffaelina Cerase (1914–1915),* second edition. Revised and corrected by Father Gerardo Di Flumeri. San Giovanni Rotondo: "Padre Pio da Pietrelcina" Editions, 1987.

———. *Letters Volume III: Correspondence With His Spiritual Daughters (1915–1923)* English version edited by Fr. Alessio Parente. San Giovanni Rotondo: "Padre Pio da Pietrelcina" Editions, 1994.

da Pobladura, Melchiorre and Alessandro da Ripabottoni, eds. *Letters Volume IV.* (Volume IV is not yet available in English. Title of Italian edition: *Padre Pio da Pietrelcina, Epistolario IV. Corrispondenza con diverse categorie di persone.* San Giovanni Rotondo: "Padre Pio da Pietrelcina" Editions, 1984.

Del Fante, Alberto. *Per la storia. Padre Pio da Pietrelcina.* Bologna: Anonima Arti Grafiche, 1950.

Festa, Giorgio. *Tra I misteri della scienza e le luci della fede.* Gaglianico: Arte Della Stampa, 1933.

Parente, Fr. Alessio, ed. *Padre Pio: Counsels.* Dublin: Padre Pio Office, 1982.

———. *Have a Good Day,* third ed. San Giovanni Rotondo: "Padre Pio da Pietrelcina" Editions, 1995.

———. *Padre Pio: Our Good Samaritan,* San Giovanni Rotondo: "Padre Pio da Pietrelcina" Editions, 1990.

———. *"Send Me Your Guardian Angel": Padre Pio.* Naples: Editions Carlo Tozza, 1984.

Ruffin, C. Bernard. *Padre Pio: The True Story.* Huntington, Ind.: Our Sunday Visitor, 1991.

Schug, John A., O.F.M. CAP. *A Padre Pio Profile.* Peterham, Mass.: St. Bede's, 1987.

Treece, Patricia. *Apparitions of Modern Saints: Appearances of Thérèse of Lisieux, Padre Pio, Don Bosco, and Others.* Cincinnati: Servant, 2001.

———. *Meet Padre Pio: Beloved Mystic, Miracle Worker, and Spiritual Guide.* Cincinnati: Servant, 2001.

———. *Nothing Short of a Miracle: God's Healing Power in Modern Society.* Manchester, N.H.: Sophia Institute, 2013.

———. *Quiet Moments With Padre Pio: 120 Daily Readings.* Cincinnati: Servant, 1999.

———. *Through the Year With Padre Pio: 365 Daily Readings.* Cincinnati: Servant, 2003.

If you enjoyed this book about Padre Pio, you may also enjoy these!

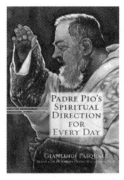

Padre Pio's Spiritual
Direction for Every Day

ISBN 978-1-61636-005-4

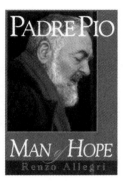

Padre Pio
Man of Hope

ISBN 978-1-56955-138-7

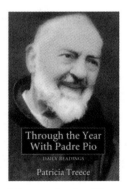

Through the Year
with Padre Pio

ISBN 978-1-56955-277-3

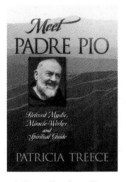

Meet Padre Pio

ISBN 978-1-56955-249-0

To order, call 800-488-0488 or visit your local bookstore.